14–19 Education
Policy, Leadership and Learning

Jacky Lumby
and Nick Foskett

SAGE Publications
London • Thousand Oaks • New Delhi

Sage Publications
1 Oliver's Yard
55 City Road
London EC1Y 1SP

SAGE Publications Inc
2455 Teller Road
Thousand Oaks, California 91320

SAGE Publications India Pvt Ltd
B-42, Panchsheel Enclave
Post Box 4109
New Delhi 110 017

Library of Congress Control Number 2004 096708

A catalogue record for this book is available from the
British Library

ISBN 1 4129 0146 4
ISBN 1 4129 0147 2 (pbk)

Index compiled by Christopher Bowring-Carr
Typeset by Dorwyn Ltd, Wells, Somerset
Printed by Gopsons Papers Ltd., India.

Contents

Figures and tables

Preface

The shifting focus of public and political attention in education is a mysterious ebb and flow of fashion. What was a central concern one year, or one decade, fades into relative obscurity as another concern, another perspective, moves into the foreground. 14–19 education is one such concern that appears suddenly to have moved centre stage, the subject of intense scrutiny and reforming activity. As with many apparently 'sudden' manifestations, the preparations have been a long time in the making. Concerns over, for example, the numbers leaving schooling with few or no qualifications, youth unemployment, the unsuitability of the qualifications gained to equip young people for twenty-first century life and work, have all surfaced in many and varied forms for decades. The recent appearance of 14–19 education as a target for policy development is the result of such concerns increasing in intensity. A rising wave of anxiety that education and training do not do right by our young people, and that the implications are (and will be) widely felt in our society has finally crashed onto the policy shore. Catastrophe theory suggests that pressures for change build over time until suddenly the critical moment is reached, the wave breaks, and what seemed inevitable and unchangeable becomes malleable and changing. The Berlin Wall falls. We believe that 14–19 education is at such a point and that there is the potential for significant change in a way which has not previously been the case; the time is right for fundamental reconsideration of what 14–19 education is for. Even more importantly, it is time to consider *who* it is for. Even a cursory glance will reveal that the needs and voice of 14–19-year-olds themselves as individuals have not figured largely in the policy debate to date.

Why should this be of interest to those who work to improve practice and reshape policy? We argue in this book that getting it right for 14–19-year-olds has implications for all of us, that the hopes of making our society more inclusive, more just and more efficient hinge on this phase of education. It is at 14–19 that corrosive divisions are finalized, between the 'successful' and the 'unsuccessful', the high status and the low status. This is hardly surprising given that policy and practice have been based for decades on division, by age, by ability, by background, by types of organization, by government department.

With the White Paper *Learning to Compete* (DfES, 1997a) came a recognition that the elements in place maybe did not add up to a satisfactory whole, that young people do not see their learning as slices of different cakes but as a continuity through their lives, and that the legislation which allows them to opt out at 16 is less relevant to many than the choices they must make for how to continue to learn or to train. Sixteen is no longer the critical point in time it may once have been. The concerns of decades have then been more sharply focused and reformulated as '14–19 education'. The implication in labelling the last two years of compulsory schooling and the first two years of post-compulsory education and training in this way signals an emphasis on achieving greater coherence in what young people and their families experience.

We argue also that young people of 14–19 are not the same in their beliefs and preferences as previous generations, and that the expectations of education and training are changing. The book maps out what is different and uniquely challenging about 14–19 education at this moment in time, the history of attempts at reform, the current experience of education and training of this age group and, finally, some of the directions and possibilities for the future. Parts of the volume will, we hope, be a valuable reference for those looking to understand how we have got to where we are. We also hope that parts will provoke, will stimulate and will demand reconsideration of the meaning and effects of current policy and practice, and will provide some ideas of how things might be different.

This book is in part powered by a commitment formed by working with young people and staff in different ways, as teachers ourselves and, latterly, as researchers. Our thanks go to the many staff and young people who have talked to us in schools and colleges for a number of years, for their frankness, their generosity and from whom we learned a great deal. We also owe a debt to our own teenage children, who brought home on a daily basis some of the realities of 14–19-year-old life and how important it is to their future as well as our own to nurture all our young people.

Jacky Lumby and Nick Foskett
University of Lincoln and University of Southampton
July 2004

Acknowledgements

The following are reproduced with permission:

Figure 9.1 Accessed on line 1 July 2004, DfES (2004a) © Crown copyright.

Table 6.1 Armitage, A., Bryant, B., Dunhill, R., Hammersley, M., Hudson, A. and Lawes, S. (1999) *Teacher and Training in Post-Compulsory Education* © McGraw-Hill Education.

Table 6.2 Armitage, A., Bryant, B., Dunhill, R., Hammersley, M., Hudson, A. and Lawes, S. (1999) *Teacher and Training in Post-Compulsory Education* © McGraw-Hill Education.

Table 6.3 From Colley, R., Hodkinson, P. and Malcolm, J. (2003): *Informality and formality in learning: a report for the Learning and Skills Research Centre*, Figure 7 p. 25. © LSRC. To read this report visit www.LSRC.ac.uk

Abbreviations

A level	Advanced level
AS	Advanced Subsidiary
AVCE	Advanced Vocational Certificate of Education
BTEC	Business and Technology Education Council
C&G	City and Guilds
CBI	Confederation of British Industry
CEE	Certificate of Extended Education
CEG	careers education and guidance
CEO	chief education officer
COVE	Centre of Vocational Excellence
CPVE	Certificate of Pre-vocational Education
CSE	Certificate of Secondary Education
CTC	city technology college
DE	Department of Employment
DES	Department of Education and Science
DfEE	Department for Education and Employment
DfES	Department for Education and Skills
DTI	Department of Trade and Industry
EPPI Centre	Evidence for Policy and Practice Information and Co-ordination Centre
FE	further education
FEFC	Further Education Funding Council
FEU	Further Education Unit
GCE	General Certificate in Education
GCSE	General Certificate of Secondary Education
GFEC	general further education college
GM	grant maintained
GNVQ	General National Vocational Qualification
HE	higher education
IAG	information advice and guidance
ICT	information and communications technology
IPPR	Institute for Public Policy Research
IT	information technology

LEA	local education authority
LLSC	Local Learning and Skills Council
LMS	Local Management of Schools
LSC	Learning and Skills Council
LSS	Learning and Skills Sector
MA	Modern Apprenticeship
MSC	Manpower Services Commission
MLD	moderate learning difficulties
NC	National Curriculum
NCC	National Curriculum Council
NCSL	National College for School Leadership
NCVQ	National Council for Vocational Qualifications
NEET	not in education, employment or training
NTO	national training organization
NVQ	National Vocational Qualification
NVQF	National Vocational Qualification Framework
O level	Ordinary level
OECD	Organization for Economic Cooperation and Development
OFSTED	Office for Standards in Education
OPC	organizational partnership and collaboration
ORF	output-related funding
PFI	Private Funding Initiative
PIC	Private Industry Council
PPP	Public Private Partnership
QCA	Qualifications and Curriculum Authority
RDA	Regional Development Agency
ROA	Record of Achievement
RSA	Royal Society of Arts
SAT	Standard Attainment Test
SCAA	School Curriculum and Assessment Authority
SEN	special educational needs
ses	socio-economic status
SLDD	specific learning difficulties and disabilities
TEC	Training and Enterprise Council
TTA	Teacher Training Agency
TVEI	Technical and Vocational Education Initiative
YCS	Youth Cohort Study
YOP	Youth Opportunities Programme
YTS	Youth Training Scheme

LEA	local education authority
LLSC	Local Learning and Skills Council
LMS	Local Management of Schools
LSC	Learning and Skills Council
LSS	Learning and Skills Sector
MA	Modern Apprenticeship
MSC	Manpower Services Commission
MLD	moderate learning difficulties
NC	National Curriculum
NCC	National Curriculum Council
NCSL	National College for School Leadership
NCVQ	National Council for Vocational Qualifications
NEET	not in education, employment or training
NTO	national training organization
NVQ	National Vocational Qualification
NVQF	National Vocational Qualification Framework
O level	Ordinary level
OECD	Organization for Economic Cooperation and Development
OfSTED	Office for Standards in Education
OIC	organizational interaction and collaboration
ORF	output-related funding
PFI	Private Finance Initiative
PIC	Private Industry Council
PPP	Public Private Partnership
QCA	Qualifications and Curriculum Authority
RDA	Regional Development Agency
ROA	Record of Achievement
RSA	Royal Society of Arts
SAT	Standard Attainment Test
SCAA	School Curriculum and Assessment Authority
SEN	special educational needs
SI	statutory instrument
SLDD	students learning difficulties and disabilities
TEC	Training and Enterprise Council
TTA	Teacher Training Agency
TVEI	Technical and Vocational Education Initiative
YCS	Youth Cohort Study
YOP	Youth Opportunities Programme
YTS	Youth Training Scheme

PART 1

SETTING THE CONTEXT

Chapter 1

14–19 education:
the high-stakes battlefield

Introduction

In a radio programme the ornithologist Bill Oddie recounted how he once saw a fox from his kitchen window and in great excitement shouted to his teenage daughter to come and look. She hurried to respond to the urgent shouts, looked out of the window and coolly asked her father, 'And this affects me how?' Writing a volume of this sort, there is a sort of parallel situation; the authors are convinced of the timeliness and excitement of the subject but recognize that potential readers will be equally cool in calculating the relevance of the content to them. We wish to argue and to convince that the focus of this volume, the education of 14–19-year-olds, is a phase of education which demands greater attention from a whole range of stakeholders and that the case for such attention is urgent and compelling. The incident also has a second relevance, in that it reflects strongly the perspective of the young person involved. In this volume too, we wish to attempt to understand how 14–19 education and training are viewed and experienced by young people themselves.

Until recently, secondary education was conceived as comprising compulsory and post-compulsory elements as distinct components, or sometimes as two age groups, 11–16 and 16–19 year olds. The idea of learners aged 14–19 forming a discrete classification has only relatively recently come into the policy and practice domains, with the first White Paper focused on this group, *Learning to Compete* (DfEE, 1997a). Education is a constantly shifting kaleidoscope, with different parts of the system and different priorities remaining on the periphery or coming into sharper focus over time. This book is founded on the belief that the myriad pieces which constitute the experience and outcomes of learning have shifted. A new pattern named '14–19 education' has emerged as a focal point and will remain a stable and influential priority for some time

3

to come. This book hopes to illuminate policy and practice for all those involved in devising policy, preparing educators and supporting the development of young people in this age group.

Look now!

The conviction that the time is ripe to take an in-depth look at 14–19 education is one of the drivers of this volume. During the 1980s and 1990s dissatisfaction with the outcomes of education was broadly shaped by the twin criticisms that young people were not being adequately prepared in their knowledge, skills and attitudes for the world of work and that standards of achievement generally were slipping (Pring, 1990). Dissatisfaction with both outputs (qualifications achieved, value-added) and outcomes (number entering employment or further education [FE]) (Chapman and Adams, 1998) has continued, fuelled by international comparisons, particularly of the number of young people failing to achieve minimum qualifications at 16 and the percentage remaining in education after 16. However, a number of factors, including changes in the demographic profile of society, global demands for higher skill levels in the workforce, flows of migrants and the disproportionate experience of poverty by children in the 3.8 million living in low-income households (Palmer et al., 2003), have increased the emphasis on education as the key for social and economic success. The changes have also compelled a more sophisticated analysis of education and the causes of perceived failures. Governments have been forced to accept that the roots of divisions and underachievement within education cannot be explained purely by blaming schools (McLean, 1995). Rather, the process of social reproduction, the ways in which those who have power and resources retain them, has become much more the target for change. There has been a sort of intensification of concern, an urgency to tackle the persistent educational underclass (OECD, 1992). In response, policy changes and initiatives have sought to reform every part of education, but 14–19 is at the heart, the nucleus of intense expectation.

The second driver of this volume is the belief that the 14–19 phase of education is not only distinctive but in some ways unique and therefore requires a dedicated perspective. We argue that it is a particularly critical fulcrum in the educational process, where learners are distinctive, where the expectations of government, young people, families and employers,

amongst others, are funnelled and competing, and that, as a consequence, 14–19 education is a battlefield where high-stakes competition
between individuals and groups results in contradiction, contest, and
confusion.

The distinctive phase

Learners

The 14–19 phase of education is distinctive in a number of ways. First,
the nature of learners is unlike those in other phases. As learners enter
their adolescent years, they are, in legislation, compelled to remain in
school. In practice young people exercise choice in absenting themselves
through truanting. They may also exhibit behaviour which results in
their exclusion by others. In 2001/02 there were 33,040 unauthorized
absences from secondary schools. The national average of 1.1 per cent
conceals variation where in some cities the absence rate is over 10 per
cent (DfES, 2003a). In the same year there were 7,740 permanent exclusions from secondary schools (DfES, 2003b). Statistics are not collected in
colleges in the same form of unauthorized absences, but the *Annual
Report* of Her Majesty's Inspectorate commenting on post-compulsory
education notes that: 'The attendance rate at all lessons observed by
inspectors was 78%. In sixth form colleges it was 85%, and in general further education and tertiary colleges 76%. All these figures are
unsatisfactory' (OFSTED, 2003, p. 1). Overall, the figures provide evidence of a large number of young people who are temporarily or
permanently outside the 14–19 education system.

Fourteen to nineteen-year-olds feel a strong sense of their growing
adulthood and wish their voice to be heard. De Pear (1997) researched
the attitudes of excluded and disaffected young people and found that
the perceived absence of adults listening to them was a factor in the
physical or psychological opting out of such learners. There is also a
growing demand for 'respect' and much evidence that many learners
believe teachers do not offer it (Bentley, 1998; Blatchford, 1996). The
generation gap between teachers and learners, not such a problem lower
down the system, comes into sharp focus (Bentley, 1998). Though the
rate of maturation obviously varies amongst individuals, within the
14–19 age range young people increasingly see themselves as adults with

a right to be heard and to exercise control over their lives and their learning. Bentley (1998, p. 80) summarizes the dilemma that in the latter part of secondary schooling, 'there is a growing disjunction between the *power* of adults and institutions and their *authority*' (original emphasis).

Awareness of the world beyond school or college also grows. The earlier connection in learners' minds between doing well at school and getting a good job strengthens (Blatchford, 1996). Contact with employment increases as part-time work is a growing element in learners' lives. Recent studies indicate that 42 per cent of 14-year-olds are in paid employment, rising to 80 per cent of 18–19-year-olds (Hodgson and Spours, 2001). The work is not necessarily confined to the weekend but is also undertaken during the school week. Such work is not a sort of hobby or minor adjunct but an essential part of young people's self-identity (Hughes, 1999; Lucas and Lammont, 1998). The need not just for financial security, but for sufficient funds to enjoy life are essential for a sense of success. However, striving for such personal success is within the context of increasing polarity within society between the haves and the have nots (Palmer et al., 2003).

A picture emerges of young people increasingly wishing to control their lives, to receive respect from other adults, to make choices according to their own preferences and not necessarily to be confined by school parameters. They may choose to spend time in paid work as a priority and they may choose not to come into school at all. Many young people have already faced life choices, changes, demands and difficulties which exceed those experienced by many adults. But this is only a partial picture. There is also evidence of the lack of experience of young people, their vulnerability in needing adult approval, and their fear, as well as relish, of adulthood. De Pear's (1997) study showed disaffected young people not only wishing their voice to be heard, but also needing affection, needing a sense of acceptance. Lumby et al.'s (2003a) study of young people in London schools presents evidence of the degree to which young people are manipulated by adults in schools, colleges and their families to support a range of expectations and vested interests. Lumby and Briggs (2002) also discovered that young people combined a strongly felt wish for independence with a fear of situations where they had too much freedom, too much responsibility. They wanted 'cushioned adulthood' (ibid., p. 61). Thus, neither the pedagogy evolved in relation to children nor the androgogy which reflects the learning style of adults may be adequate to the needs of the 14–19 age group who are neither fully children nor fully adult. In this sense the 14–19 age group is unique and presents the first contradiction. How can young people be offered the independence and choice they increasingly demand, and yet be protected from the ill effects of such independence which they themselves fear as well as desire?

Government

The sources of government expectations lie with a plethora of beliefs, assumptions, fears and aspirations. At a European level, the 1992 meeting of Organization for Economic Cooperation and Development (OECD) Education Ministers wished education to develop skills to support employment, but also personal and social skills such as 'curiosity, independence and leadership, ability to co-operate, tolerance, industriousness, and problem solving under conditions of uncertainty' (OECD, 1992, p. 104). Within the UK, this desire to meet both economic and social aims has been explicit in Labour's 'Third Way' orientation, seeing education as powering both social justice and an internationally competitive economy. The two, of course, are not independent of each other, the stability of the economy and of society being mutually reinforcing.

McLean (1995) highlights the reason why upper secondary education is of particular interest to governments in offering opportunities to engineer society and the economy through a differentiated curriculum in a way which is not possible lower down the system. Younger children follow a largely undifferentiated curriculum to achieve foundation skills and knowledge:

> After 10 to 14 years of education, the range of attainment of 16 year-olds is too great for them to be taught to one standard. Particular gifts of all young people, specialised as well as of a general kind, need to be developed … Artistic, physical, manual as well as particular intellectual talents need space to flower. Yet general education to basic levels needs to be maintained by all. (McLean, 1995, p. 147)

McLean places the alteration at 16, but the choice of GCSE options suggests the point of change as earlier, at 14. Differentiating what is taught much more than for 5–13-year-olds, opens up the prospect of manipulating the curriculum to achieve government aims. It is an invitation to experiment which has proved irresistible for some decades. In particular, successive governments have grappled with the ambivalent aims of providing success for all and also a classification system for the benefit of higher education (HE), employers and wider society.

Classification takes priority as 14–19 education is shaped above all by assessment (Bowring-Carr and West-Burnham, 1997; Lumby 2001a). Foucault (1977) analyses examination systems as providing surveillance and punishment, ensuring a restricted entry to the elite and penalties for the remainder. This has certainly been the experience of 14–19-year-olds with half of 16-year-olds failing to achieve the target five or more A*–C at GCSE in 2001/02 (DfES, 2003c), and high rates of both failure and dropout in A levels and GNVQs by 19 (Audit Commission/OFSTED, 1993; OFSTED, 2003). McLean (1995, p. 142) contrasts the approaches of the Soviet Union, in attempting to ensure achievement by all of a minimum standard by a system of sanctions against parents and students, the USA which provides a 'comprehensive curriculum of academic, vocational, social adjustment and recreational subjects' taught in a style which encourages articulate and confident students, and the European approach which sets minimum standards and then lets the majority fail to reach them.

In the UK the subject content of the curriculum has not changed very much since the start of the twentieth century (Pring, 1990). Adjustments in education have been largely driven for decades by the repeated ritualistic expression of concern about A levels, their narrowness and academic orientation, followed by, until recently, a refusal to change them. In essence, reform has mainly comprised a series of initiatives to sort young people onto 'tracks' and then provide discrete solutions – Youth Opportunities, Youth Training Programme, Modern Apprenticeships and so on, which largely have not touched the mainstream 14–19 curriculum (see Chapter 2).

Fourteen to nineteen is also of particular interest to government in that it crosses the point of 'massification' of the system (Hodgson and Spours, 2003). If skill levels are to be raised in the whole population, persuasion to stay on after the compulsory phase must be laid prior to 16 and the offering post-16 must be sufficiently attractive. In this way, it could be argued that success in national aims to secure an appropriate workforce hinges on success in the 14–19 phase.

The potential contradiction in both the existing arrangements and in aims for the future is evident. How can 14–19 education provide an experience of success for the whole population while simultaneously differentiating people according to levels of ability and skills predilection? This is the second contradiction.

Families

The perspective of families differs from those of governments. The over-whelming concern for middle-class families is not success for all, but success for their own children. The aim is to maintain or increase social and cultural capital. The impetus is intense and anything that threatens or impedes is resisted (Ball, 2003). For working-class families education presents more complicated choices, as young people and their families use education as a route to another class, or as a means of confirming their identity within their family's current class and culture (Reay, 2001a). Families are then 'the motor of inequality' (Ball, 2003, p. 4). As McLean (1995) points out, even in Japan where enrolment in schools is strictly by ability, and strategies such as moving residence, for example, will not gain entry, rich parents still have resource to crammer schools to offer an edge to their children. Globally, the curriculum is designed from the perspective of the dominant class and is therefore unlikely to be subject to change which will threaten that dominance. In the UK the long history of middle-class resistance to changing A levels is an obvious example (Hodgson and Spours, 2003). There is little that can be done to circumvent the rich and powerful from securing advantage for their children.

Young people themselves are complicit in maintaining class division. When interviewing young people as to their choice of programme and place of study post-16, Lumby and Briggs (2002) found repeated reference to status and prestige as highly desirable commodities. Young people themselves were instrumental in primarily seeing education as the means to secure long-term advantage in terms of jobs and income. They had bought into credentialism and were anxious to secure qualifications which would act as currency for entry to the highest status institutions. In this way, they were curators of class divisions as enacted through the different status accorded to different education programmes and institutions. For some, far from wishing to erode differential prestige, buying into or opting out of the hierarchy of prestige is an essential source of their self-esteem and 'street cred' with others (Lumby et al., 2003b) enacted through choosing to study wherever is 'fashionable'. Foskett et al. (2003, p. 6) explore the idea of 'fashionability' which: 'in this context is seen as the primacy of particular choices on the basis of their perceived acceptability to specific social groups, where that primacy is based on subjective judgements of value rather than, necessarily, objective measures of value'. The flow towards the perceived greatest prestige and status are thus embedded in cultures which aim for or avoid particular locations for study or training.

Fourteen to nineteen is therefore the phase where staying in or moving class is most crucially negotiated. The examinations at 16 and 18 each act not just as gateways to further study/training, to employment or to becoming subject to the curt term 'NEET' (not in education, employment or training), but also to a position in relation to others. If the resulting position is not as hoped, the consequences may be lifelong. Although it is possible to recover lost opportunities by returning to study in later life, for many, the 14–19 phase is an irrecoverable rite of passage where success or failure impacts on life chances in a profound way. It is a high-stakes conflict area, between individuals, classes, families and government.

Employers

Much of the change suggested by government is justified in terms of the need to supply a highly skilled workforce and to eradicate 'skills shortage'. However, the analysis of the current and future availability of appropriate employees and possible responses to the perceived situation are highly contested. Some argue that the mooted relationship between the skills level of the workforce and economic success is not proven (Keep, 1999; Wolf, 2002) The extent and nature of the 'skills shortage' is also disputed (Steedman, 2002). Nevertheless, employers themselves, or rather those that speak for them, have persisted in expressing dissatisfaction with the preparedness of young people for employment in their knowledge, skills and attitudes (CBI, 2002a; 2002b). The 14–19 phase is of great interest as the interface between education and employment. However, the perspective of employers is somewhat different from government, families and young people themselves. Despite their criticism of the existing system, UK employers have not invested in education to the extent of some other European countries (McLean, 1995) and have preferred to leave the government to provide the necessary outlay. The captive audience of 14–19-year-olds is perceived as a simpler and cheaper way of training the workforce than training or retraining adults, where the costs must be borne by employers and/or the individual him/herself, and also avoids having to take responsibility for the deficiencies or otherwise of the workforce.

While the government persists in using qualifications as the driver of change, adjusting what is studied and how it is assessed, employers are less

interested in this tactic. First, Steedman suggests that 'a scan of job adver-
tisements in Britain reveals an almost total absence of reference to
qualifications' (2002, p. 25). Secondly, concerns as expressed by the CBI
(2002a) reflect irritation with persistent change. Their stated need is for certification of basic skills, differentiation between vocational and academic
qualifications, and a grading system which is sufficiently discriminating to
allow finely tuned selection of employees. The lack of coherence in such
requirements has been noted, as has the fact that there is no such thing as
'employers': 'The needs and concerns of big and small, manufacturing and
finance, local, national and multinational, and traditional, service and
high-tech businesses are not the same. Industrialists, or those who speak for
them, do not necessarily speak with one voice' (Ball, 1999, p. 61).

There is, consequently, a range of opinion and demands. However, the
focus tightens and expectation heightens at that first moment of interface between the world of school and the world of work, the 14–19
period. If all is not as they wish, it is here that employers will feel it most
strongly. The needs of the economy cannot be matched by the rate of
change in education (Keep, 1999). Nevertheless, the 14–19 phase is perceived as the pressure point for shorter-term outputs to meet the
requirements of the economy, despite the fact that there are arguments
in the literature that such outcomes can never be achieved. Here therefore is a third contradiction.

Higher education

The government has set a target for 50 per cent of all 19-year-olds to
enter higher education by 2010. Consequently universities and other
organizations offering higher education could be seen as one of the
largest 'consumers' of 14–19 education. Increasingly, the path to higher
education is seen as the primary indicator of success with all other paths
a second best alternative. Consequently, higher education holds much
power as the gatekeeper to economic success and prestige for individuals
and their families (Lumby et al., 2003a). The power converts to influence, as schools, colleges and individuals all strive to achieve what
higher education sees as currency for entry. The universities, particularly,
have a stranglehold on the currency of qualifications. Reforms in content
and accreditation in 14–19 education have remained peripheral if higher
education does not value the results. For example, young people under-

taking key skills found little interest in universities in the resulting qualifications (Lumby and Briggs, 2002). Many were forced to undertake key skills accreditation against their wishes in order for their school or college to secure funding, only to find that the resulting qualifications were not valued. Advanced Level Certificate in Education, by contrast, has retained its currency, despite decades of dissatisfaction with the qualification, because higher education demands it. If higher education does not agree to change in the curriculum and accreditation system, then change is impeded and, generally, higher education does not agree. Higher education's control of the system ensures that 14–19 education is shaped primarily for the half of young people who are intended for higher education, not the half who are not.

The 14–19 phase

In summary, expectations for the 14–19 phase are more specific than in earlier phases. Young people, government, parents and employers, and other stakeholders such as higher education all have very particular outcomes they wish from this phase of education and, therefore, there are a greater range of more explicit and contradictory requirements. The increased desire from a range of players to impose what they feel will meet their requirements clashes head-on with the burgeoning desire for self-direction from young people. Fourteen to nineteen-year-olds see themselves as adults with a right to make their own decisions whilst at the same time other stakeholders are anxious to impose a structure and activities that will meet their own expectations, not necessarily those of young people.

Consequently, 14–19 is a battlefront where education meets the outside world. It is the interface point where the realities of having to deal with the need to get a job and take a place in society come much more closely into contact with education and, because of this, it seems a last-ditch opportunity to engineer people to meet requirements. Young people are to some degree a captive audience and relatively powerless and inexperienced to resist. It is therefore, at the last gasp of the compulsory phase, a final opportunity for the exercise of power.

It may be that given the environment described, 14–19 will remain a 'cannot do' rather than a 'can do' phase. The expectations of each group of stakeholders may be impossible to meet. For example, Keep (1999) has argued that it is impossible to fulfil the diverse needs of the amorphous group called 'employers'. The aims of government may be equally problematic. As an example, much of the current movement in policy and practice is to challenge the low esteem in which vocational education and training is held, despite the fact that across most cultures the lower status of vocational education is deeply embedded in the culture of the family (King, 1993), and as Wolf (2002) argues, with good reason, as vocational training/qualifications leads generally to lower levels of income. Changing such deeply embedded beliefs may not be feasible in the short to medium term, and perhaps even long term. Families wish for success for their children in the teeth of a system designed in part to distinguish success and failure. For each group in its own right, disappointment is likely. When the contradiction between the aims of the various groups is added as a further layer, the 14–19 phase is inevitably going to be perceived as failing in the eyes of various groups. The way forward, therefore, may be not to attempt to reform the system to reach impossible targets but to reconsider expectations. The Education Ministers of the OECD recognized this over a decade ago (OECD, 1992), though the impact of this recognition on policy is not yet apparent.

For decades, despite the rhetoric, nothing radical has been attempted. The changes which have been implemented have often not worked as intended, and/or have not achieved what was expected (Keep, 1999). In its analysis of the issues that need to be addressed by 14–19 reform, the Tomlinson Committee (Working Group on 14–19 Reform, 2003) identified seven symptoms of weakness in the current arrangements for education and training within this age group – high drop-out rates; low achievement; the uncertain currency of some qualifications; lack of breadth of study; low personal rewards associated with some vocational qualification achievements; high levels of illiteracy and innumeracy amongst adults; and the widespread perception amongst employers and higher education that young people lack key generic skills and attributes needed for employment or higher level study. Existing patterns of inequality have persisted as governments tinker with the supply side, but the demand side remains untouched (Lumby and Wilson, 2003). Gains have been made in raising the level of achievement but, nevertheless, a sense of failure remains. There are structural, cultural and curriculum issues which remain unresolved. The disparity of status between different routes, different qualifications, different types of education and training provider remains intact. Even for those who succeed in terms of achieving high-status qualifications, there is a sense that something important has been lost. The 'successful' young person is in 'pursuit of credentials in the construction of the marketable self' (Furman and Shields, 2003, p. 21). While there is no suggestion that pursuing a course which assures employment and economic security is anything but sensible, if that is the primary aim of education, it suggests an impoverished system, focused narrowly, which cuckoo-like, has displaced other aims to do with nurturing the moral, cultural and spiritual dimensions. Preparation for employment (for those that can achieve it) takes primacy over preparation for living.

These issues are played out in the structural divisions within the system. Although the new discourse is on 14–19 education, it is clear that deeply embedded divisions between pre- and post-16 persist. Physically the system is divided, with more young people in colleges post-16 than remain in schools (see Chapter 6) and a further proportion attending work-based training. Funding pre- and post-16 is controlled by different bodies and disbursed in different ways. Merely labelling the experience of young people '14–19 education' has no effect on the system's coherence or effectiveness. Much, much more will be needed.

Aims of the volume

We have argued that the distinctive characteristics of the 14–19 phase are

- intensity
- contradiction
- conflict
- confusion

and that, because of these characteristics, the phase is in some sense doomed to remain perceived as failing unless a fresh look is taken at what it is to achieve and for whom. The already high stakes have recently been ratcheted up further by government plans for more radical change. The White Paper (DFEE, 1997a) followed by the government review of 14–19 education led by Tomlinson signalled a period of more fundamental change than has been the case for some decades. This volume is therefore timely in considering in detail the policy and practice of education and training for 14–19-year-olds.

The book focuses on this age group in England, as policy and practice in both Wales and Scotland differ, and will have the following primary aims:

1. To explore the social, economic, political and educational context within which 14–19 education and training has evolved and is evolving.
2. To provide an overview of the principle issues in 14–19 education and training, reflecting the differing perspectives of key players such as the government, young people, schools, colleges and the labour market.
3. To map the policy changes which have affected 14–19 education and training in the latter half of the twentieth century and particularly the 1990s to date.
4. To analyse teaching and learning and curriculum developments in 14–19 education and training since the 1980s to date.
5. To outline some policy alternatives for the future development of 14–19 education and training and their possible implications.
6. To illuminate the implications for developing practice within schools, colleges and support services.

In order to meet each of these aims the book is structured first to explore the context since 1979 with the advent of the Thatcher government, outlining both the structural and curriculum changes that have taken place. The second part focuses on the learning experience, investigating how teaching, qualifications and assessment have changed, and how this relates to the perceived embedded divide between vocational and academic tracks. The third part offers ideas on the implications for those structures and activities which support the phase, partnership, resources and leadership of education and training. The final chapter explores what the future might look like, or rather what possible futures there might be for our 14–19-year-olds. The hope is that the volume will provide knowledge and support reflection for those who are working with this age group, but that it will also stimulate policy-makers. At the European level, the inflation and dissonance in the expectations of education and training has been recognized as a significant barrier to progress. At the local UK level, a number of factors including the levelling of rise in achievement and participation (Hodgson and Spours, 2003), the debacle of the Curriculum 2000 examination fiasco in 2002, the growing nervousness about shortages of skilled craftspeople, have all signalled the need for more fundamental reform.

Government policy embraces a rhetoric of inclusion, learner-centredness and breadth in education. Whatever the intention, the effect of government policy over the last two decades has been somewhat different, to turn 'young people into commodities which are much sought after by the various providers' (Unwin, 2002, p. 19). Correspondence theory suggests that schools mirror the workplace (Butterfield, 1998). The exclusion or marginalization of some learners may reflect the evolution of core and peripheral workers (Handy, 1994). Just as parts of the population will find themselves picking up jobs on the margins, temporary, ill paid and undervalued, so learners in schools are commodities which show a division into central and peripheral.

Ritual is the means by which society deals with emotions and events which may be unpleasant, unacceptable or inexplicable. Long-standing patterns of language and actions are used to deflect, conceal or channel what cannot be openly displayed or allowed unfettered expression. The debate about 14–19 education has something of the nature of ritual. Systems are ordered under the chant of 'learner-centred' while carefully considering the needs of a whole range of stakeholders other than individual learners. Ritual is designed to ameliorate feelings. In the case of 14–19 education, discussing meeting learners' needs makes everyone feel better, even while they pursue interests which relate to their individual or organizational interests. Future generations of 14–19-year-olds deserve more and demand greater clarity about aims and how they are to be achieved in an arena where vested interests exert powerful distorting forces. It is hoped that this volume will contribute to negotiating the minefield of 14–19 education by exploring further the contradiction, conflict and confusion at this period of potential radical change, and by asking readers to take a reality check on the education of 14–19-year-olds.

Chapter 2
Riding the waves of policy

When the Thatcher government was elected in 1979, education and training in England operated a system largely established by the 1944 Education Act. Schools and further education were under the direct control of local education authorities (LEAs) and, theoretically, provided a locally based and focused education and training system. While schools had been in the political and public spotlight through comprehensivization, further education pre-1979 was what Gleeson (1996) has described as the 'Cinderella' of the education system, with little serious attention from government (local or national). Thatcherism ushered in an era of radical change. The 'post-war settlement' (Salter and Tapper, 1981) in which the tacit agreement that policy and practice in the public sector would be left to the professionals within those services (Chitty, 1996), was abandoned, and replaced by a centralizing and reforming agenda from government. The relative tranquillity of the educational policy climate of the 1970s was replaced by a stormy period of frequently destabilizing change that continues through to today.

The context for policy change was the view that the economic malaise of the 1970s and early 1980s was in significant part the result of the failure of the education and training system to deliver a skilled workforce to compete in the global economy. This considers education and training from a human capital perspective, with individuals primarily a resource to be invested in pursuit of national economic goals. Hence the generation of a trained, flexible future workforce is a key aim of the education and training 'business', 'supporting economic growth by promoting a competitive, efficient and flexible labour market' (Rajan et al., 1997, p. 2). Tuckett (1997), for example, emphasizes that there is a marked economic advantage for societies with skilled, adaptable and learning workforces in an increasingly global economy. In a context of little historical change in the system for three decades, and a government inspired by a vision of economic revitalization and challenged by high levels of (particularly youth) unemployment, it was inevitable that education and training would be seized upon as a key tool for social and economic change. This chapter outlines the chronology of 14–19 policy since 1979.

Policy shifts – turbulence or fundamental change?

A common view in education is that those working in the sector have been the victims of innovation overload (Goulding et al., 1998). This reflects a vision of continuous change, of the demand for new systems before previous waves of change have had a chance to become embedded. In reality this turbulence can be seen as having a distinctive structure and pattern rather than being simply, as frequently perceived by practitioners, a commitment to change for change's sake as a deliberate attempt to destabilize the system to enable politically motivated modifications to be introduced. In taking a macro-scale view of this turbulence we might characterize the evolution of the 14–19 sector since 1979 in terms of three waves of change, each focused on a specific dimension of the education and training system, each seeking to address some of the perceived failings of the other waves. It would be naive, of course, to believe that any government has long-term vision that planned these waves over a quarter of a century. Nevertheless, there has been a strong pattern of development that has been sequential and has transcended changes in government, and these three waves may be characterized as:

• wave 1 – initiatives and agencies for change
• wave 2 – structural change
• wave 3 – curriculum change.

The waves have not been sequential in a strict 'end on' sense in that they have overlapped and been interwoven. All persist to some extent through to the present. However, the initiation of each can be identified as the principal drive of specific periods of time, and their ascendancy, zenith and decline can be traced through the landscape of 14–19.

Wave 1 – initiatives and agencies for change

At the beginning of the Thatcher era, education and training were seen by government to have failed to deliver the economic benefits to the nation that were considered necessary (Callaghan, 1976). Initial moves to redress this problem focused strongly on youth training, since youth unemployment was regarded as the most important priority for action. The chosen strategy was to charge the responsibility for change to government agencies and to promote new initiatives to deliver the desired outcomes. Three distinctive strategies can be identified within this.

First, the education business in itself was regarded as unable to deliver the reforms so essential to improvement, and even within government the capacity and capability of the Department of Education and Science (DES) to deliver effective change on its own was strongly doubted. Development and change in the sector, therefore, became the responsibility of three government departments. While the DES still played a key role, the contribution of the Department of Employment (DE) and of the Department of Trade and Industry (DTI) were seen to be essential – education and training were identified as a key contributor to the economic profile of Britain, and so the needs of business, commerce and the economy were to be at least as important as broader educational needs.

Secondly, the ability of government departments themselves to deliver change that would prioritize the needs of the economy was strongly questioned (Cantor et al., 1995). As a result, increasing authority for planning and delivering change was placed in the hands of a number of quasi-autonomous, non-governmental organizations (quangos), whose membership and terms of reference were driven by the political aspirations of the Cabinet. With a priority for action, and an accountability that has been frequently questioned (for example, Morris, 1994), quangos emerged to act as key agencies of change, perhaps most significantly illustrated through the Manpower Services Commission (MSC).

The MSC was established in 1973 to advise government on training, skills and workforce development. Its report to government in 1977 on *Young People and Work* (the Holland Report) (MSC, 1977) led to the creation of the Youth Opportunities Programme (YOP) which supported work experience and preparation courses for unemployed young people. With the advent of the Thatcher government, the MSC became a key agency of change, and was charged with developing policy and practice in the field of training and skills. Many of the key proposals shaping change in the early 1980s emanated from the MSC. These included, for example, their paper *A New Training Initiative: An Agenda for Action* (MSC, 1981), which proposed the training agenda for government for the rest of the decade, and the proposals for the Technical and Vocational Education Initiative (TVEI) in 1982. By 1984 its status was such that the White Paper *Training for Jobs* (DES, 1984) proposed that the MSC should become in effect the national training agency, a role it fulfilled until the early 1990s, despite absorption into the Department of Employment in 1988, and its change of title to the Training Commission and then the Training Agency.

Thirdly, the focus was strongly on the vocational arena of training. The rise of the vocational agenda was set in train, as the key priority was to raise the profile of vocational pathways and qualifications as a mechanism for increasing skill levels within the labour market. This had two effects on the existing system, in that the academic curriculum post-16 was left largely untouched, bolstered by a continuing support for the 'gold standard' of A level examinations, and the school sector experienced relatively little impact. While the school curriculum had been strongly criticized since the Great Debate of 1976, this was seen as a less important focus than the vocational arena, and the pursuit of change here was rather slower. In this way the separation of the pre-16 and post-16 arenas was strongly emphasized.

The flow of initiatives came thick and fast. The Youth Opportunities Programme was but the first of many approaches. In 1979 the Further Education Unit (FEU), a quango established in 1977 to advise on developments in FE, published *A Basis for Choice* (known colloquially as ABC) (FEU, 1979), promoting a skills-based curriculum in schools and colleges to underpin vocational training. This emphasis on skills was underlined by the MSC's *A New Training Initiative: An Agenda for Action* in 1981, and three initiatives emerged in the period 1982–85 in response to these perspectives:

1. the Technical and Vocational Education Initiative (TVEI), designed to provide a broad introduction to the world of work, enterprise and skills across the 14–18 age group as a collaborative venture between schools, colleges and employer organizations
2. the Youth Training Scheme (YTS), which replaced the YOP in 1983 to provide more effective training for young people moving into vocational areas after leaving school at 16.

3. the Certificate of Pre-vocational Education (CPVE), designed as a programme to be delivered to low achievers who stayed on in school or college post-16, to provide a broad introduction to the world of work and employment.

By the mid-1980s a range of initiatives was in operation, therefore, which defined the character of training and represented the most dominant period of the wave of agencies and initiatives. However, as the political attention shifted to address the needs of schools in the second half of the decade, the initiatives declined, were transferred to other organizations and either disappeared or were replaced. The TVEI had perhaps the longest impact, leaving a legacy of co-operative working between schools and colleges and a raised profile for work-focused learning, before disappearing in the early 1990s. YTS, which had been subject to many of the criticisms that had confounded the YOP, was replaced by Youth Training in 1989. The CPVE was only of limited success, with low student take-up, and disappeared in the context of the vocational curriculum changes of the early 1990s.

By 1989 the emphasis began to shift away from agencies and initiatives. Both concepts remained in part, in that, for example, much of the development of FE in the 1990s was placed in the hands of new quangos such as the Training and Enterprise Councils (TECs) and the Further Education Funding Council (FEFC). However, their role was linked to a new approach to reform, tied to restructuring and to curriculum change as the vehicles of change. These represent the second and third waves of change.

Wave 2 – structural change

The developments of the 1980s had eschewed fundamental structural and organizational change, and the pattern of institutions and their funding and management remained much as they had for three decades. Minor changes had included the freeing of colleges by the 1985 Further Education Act to generate income beyond that from local authority allocation. However, in the space of five years (1988–93) the sector was transferred by statutory change into an environment of autonomy, self-management and competition. This reflected a perspective from government that imbuing education with a quasi-commercial structure and market accountability would produce a more efficient and responsive sector, able to expand provision yet reduce unit costs.

The 1988 Education Reform Act had two key thrusts – the introduction of the National Curriculum in schools (see below), and the establishment of delegated financial responsibility to schools in the context of the creation of a quasi-market (Le Grand, 1990) through the establishment of Local Management of Schools (LMS). The link that was directly established between student numbers and school income created a strongly competitive environment between institutions. In the context of the present analysis, competition for pupils at age 16 brought schools and colleges into a competitive market.

While colleges felt the direct impact of the 1988 Act through the effect on competition with schools, the period of greatest turbulence in post-16 emerged in the wake of the 1992 Further and Higher Education Act. The 1992 Act fundamentally transformed the organization of 16–19 in England. Although direct LEA control had been removed by the delegation of financial and management authority to FE colleges by the 1988 Education Reform Act, the 1992 Act established 16–19 institutions as independent corporations with effect from 1993. Sixth form colleges, which had remained within the schools sector post-1988, became part of the FE sector, and funding responsibility was transferred to the new Further Education Funding Council. The landscape of the FE sector which still exists today was the outcome of this change – a sector of some 450 colleges, ranging from small almost monotechnic institutions (for example, colleges of agriculture or art) to large regional colleges with many campuses and a wide range of provision not only in academic and vocational provision to 16–19-year-olds, but also in other fields including higher education.

Incorporation was accompanied by the unleashing of strong forces of marketization. Although post-compulsory education has always, de facto, operated in an arena of choice and market forces, FEFC funding models introduced strong competition. In accordance with the government policy of increasing participation, the FEFC required the sector to increase student recruitment by some 28 per cent in the period from 1992/93 to 1996/97, while at the same time applying an annual efficiency gain in the level of per capita funding. Colleges were required to achieve 'the instrumental objectives of economy, efficiency and effectiveness (the three 'E's')' (Farnham, 1993, p. 241) in a highly competitive arena. That competition was, of course, not confined to competition between FE sector colleges. The need to recruit additional students brought colleges into competition with schools across 16–19 provision, and the dismantling (and, in many cases, destruction) of existing relationships between schools and colleges that might have been a basis for integrated 14–19 planning was inevitable and rapid (Gewirtz et al., 1995).

In parallel to the reorganization of colleges came the establishment of new statutory organizations to lead the regional funding, planning and management of training, the Training and Enterprise Councils (TECs). Training and Enterprise Councils were established in 1991, based on a model of similar organizations in the USA (the Private Industry Councils [PICs]) as private limited companies with Boards dominated by representatives of local business. These 82 regional companies represented the most formal mechanism to date of attempts to integrate training into the domain and responsibility of commerce with a strong accountability to local labour market needs. Their responsibilities spread across youth training for 16–19-year-olds, training for work for unemployed adults, work-related further education in colleges and, most recently, the management of the modern apprenticeship schemes introduced in the wake of the Dearing review (Dearing, 1996). Their initial positive welcome was rapidly overtaken by increasing criticism related to overly bureaucratic organization, limited experience of education and training amongst Board members and senior managers, and significant financial difficulties, and ultimately their replacement by local Learning and Skills Councils from April 2001.

Following the structural reorganization of colleges, attention moved to the perceived need to integrate the previously separate environments of training and education. At government level the departments for education and employment were merged into a new Department for Education and Employment (DfEE) in July 1995. Integration also occurred in relation to the formal control of curriculum. The curriculum in schools, a largely academic focus, had been under the responsibility of the School Curriculum and Assessment Authority (SCAA), while the vocational curriculum had been under the control of the National Council for Vocational Qualifications (NCVQ), established in 1986 to develop a national structure and system for competence-based National Vocational Qualifications (NVQs). In 1997 these bodies merged to form a single national curriculum advisory body with considerable powers to direct and modify the curriculum in all fields, the Qualifications and Curriculum Authority (QCA).

Reorganization of structures and systems is a common consequence of political change, and the structures outlined above were a key reform focus for the new Labour government after 1997. Labour's priority of raising skill levels, increasing participation in education and training, and widening participation to social groups currently eschewing FE (and HE), was clarified in the Green Paper *The Learning Age: A Renaissance for a New Britain* (DfEE, 1998), which in turn reflected the recommendations of the Kennedy Report (Kennedy, 1997), the Fryer Report (National Advisory Group for Continuing Education and Lifelong Learning, 1997), and the Dearing *Review of Qualifications for 16–19 Year Olds* (Dearing, 1996). These high-profile reports built on the work of the Social Exclusion Unit, and gave further momentum to the processes of structural change focused on the integration of education and training across the post-16 sector. In 1999 the DfEE was renamed as the Department for Education and Skills (DfES), and the funding and management of 16–19 education and training was integrated from 2000. The FEFC and the regional TECs were replaced by a national Learning and Skills Council (LSC) and 47 local LSCs, and the 16–19 phase traditionally described as further education was renamed as the Learning and Skills Sector.

Wave 3 – challenging the curriculum

The school curriculum for 14–16-year-olds in 1979 was dominated by the schism between high-status General Certificate in Education (GCE) Ordinary level courses (O levels) for the most able 20 per cent, and low-status Certificate of Secondary Education (CSE) programmes targeted on the next 40 per cent of the ability range. The curriculum reflected the grammar school/secondary modern system that, despite its disappearance in most parts of the country during the development of comprehensive schools in the late 1960s and early 1970s, strongly drove the organization of teaching and learning. The curriculum was academic in content with little conceded to the needs of vocational education. The majority of school leavers had few qualifications, and the bottom 40 per cent of the achievement range were condemned to leaving compulsory education with little or no evidence of achievement.

The challenge to review education and training had arisen most significantly from James Callaghan's Ruskin College speech of October 1976 which 'brought education into the full light of public debate, giving education a position of prominence on public agendas' (Williams, 1992, p. 2). Four specific directions of development of the curriculum can be identified over the ensuing two decades – the emerging vocational curriculum; the evolution of academic pathways through GCSE and the National Curriculum; the prioritization of skills development; and the attempt to integrate academic and vocational curricula into a coherent system.

The development of the vocational curriculum paralleled initially the emphasis on training by the early agencies and initiatives. The National Council for Vocational Qualifications, established in 1986, was charged with creating a National Vocational Qualification Framework (NVQF) built around competence-based National Vocational Qualifications. The purpose of this strategy was to raise the proportion of the workforce with formal vocational qualifications at all levels. National Vocational Qualifications mostly provided qualifications earned predominantly in the workplace. However, the need to introduce and develop vocational understanding, awareness and skills in the classroom for young people prior to leaving formal education led to the introduction in 1992 of General National Vocational Qualifications (GNVQs). These were designed to provide equivalence with GCSEs (intermediate GNVQs) and A levels (Advanced GNVQs). The response to GNVQs was positive and most post-16 colleges and many schools embraced the development. A significant part of their popularity lay in the gradual shift within their requirements towards 'academic' content and away from vocational skills and knowledge, and the decline in the centrality of competency-based assessment. While enhancing their esteem in competition with traditional academic qualifications, this in part undermined the original intent of promoting vocational development in formal education. Furthermore, despite their popularity, perception that GNVQ represented a less credible pathway and qualification than GCSEs or A levels remained strong both amongst education professionals and the wider public.

A central aim of the Thatcher government was the introduction of a single, integrated school-leaver qualification. The General Certificate in Secondary Education (GCSE) was introduced in 1986 (first examined in 1988), and emphasized the measurement of positive achievement by pupils at 16 against a wider range of assessment criteria. While achieving the aim of integration, however, GCSE ensured the continuation of a curriculum for 14–16-year-olds based on the academic tradition. This was further underlined in the National Curriculum, introduced between 1988 and 1991, which established for the first time the detailed prescription of the curriculum of compulsory education from 5 to 16. The proposals for Key Stage 4 of the National Curriculum, serving 14–16-year-olds, simply adopted the now established GCSE structure and, although later modifications reduced the range of statutory requirements, schools remained tied to an academic curriculum for all.

Since 1997 some erosion of that academic prominence has begun to emerge. Disapplication has clearly enabled some pupils to step away from inappropriate academic courses, and the facility to enable some Key Stage 4 pupils to undertake work-related courses and programmes both in school and in further education colleges has begun to break down the barriers. However, the emergence of some vocational GCSEs from 2002 has again sought to place vocational education in an academic framework. The school curriculum remains an academic arena for most.

The rhetoric of integrating the vocational and academic curricula for 14–19-year-olds has been a strong theme. The strength of allegiance to A levels, however, has always proved a barrier to evolution and change. Proposals for the broadening of the A level curriculum by the Higginson Committee (DES, 1988) were rejected by the government, and the recurring theme of a baccalaureate system for 16–19 (for example, Institute for Public Policy Research, 1990) has had little impact. The pursuit of parity of esteem between vocational and academic pathways has been through the reform of vocational qualifications and routes rather than through significant reform of A level, and the consequence has been a continual shift of the vocational to become more academic in nature. The introduction of Curriculum 2000, however, brought together academic and vocational qualifications for the first time in a single framework, while retaining the academic centrality of A levels. Development towards an integrated system has been strongly promoted. Hodgson and Spours (1997; 1999), for example, contend that it is in the lack of integration of the vocational and academic elements of curriculum that the key problems of 14–19 can be found.

The chronology of the 14–19 sector described here provides a clear image of the turbulence which has characterized the sector, and has sought to demonstrate how that turbulence has reflected three key waves of development since 1979. All three waves remain active, and all have contributed to the changing picture over the period. In the current context the influence of a range of agencies is apparent, including, for example, the national and regional Learning and Skills Council(s), the Teacher Training Agency (TTA), the Qualifications and Curriculum Authority, the Social

Exclusion Unit and the Learning and Skills Development Agency. Structural change and curriculum change continue to be considered through, for example, the proposals for revisions to the 14–19 curriculum of the Tomlinson Committee. It is unlikely that the degree of turbulence will slow significantly, even though the rhetoric of continuing change is, in part, the pursuit of a successful and stable system.

Reality check?

The narrative of periods of intense change has two forms. First, there is the narrative that evolves through the direct subjective experiences of those involved. This accumulates in a continuous way and is the product of experience, of current professional and institutional discourse, and is frequently shaped by the 'spin' that professional and political stakeholders choose to place on events and motives. Secondly, there is the narrative that can be viewed in retrospect by a more objective analysis, when the demands and priorities of particular moments can be seen better in the context of larger-scale changes. The two narratives may coincide, and in the context of 14–19 over the period since 1979 any analysis will identify the intensity (for example, the rise and fall of GNVQs), the contradictions (for example, the constraint of choice by marketization), the conflict (for example, between schools and colleges in competing for 16-year-old students) and the confusion in the system. Alternatively, they may not, where the rhetoric of this history identifies perspectives that have been frequently unchallenged as fundamental assumptions, but which on reanalysis show themselves to be at best questionable and at worst untenable. To provide a reality check we focus on four such orthodoxies that are commonly attributed to the waves of policy but that do not stand up to close reflection.

The first myth is that 14–19 has been characterized by radical and continuous change which has produced a fundamentally different landscape for young people and for those working in the sector. Change has two distinctive elements. At a superficial level change is a state in which 'the way things are done' is modified, on time scales ranging from days to years. Systems and processes may be altered in response to evolutionary change resulting from evaluation and striving for improvement. Alternatively, they may alter by stepwise change when a new way of doing things is introduced by legislation or by professional authority. Changing the way things are done, however, does not necessarily change either the ultimate outputs of the system or the underlying principles that characterize the sector. These principles lie in the cultural and professional values and the societal expectations that underpin the system at the macro-scale. Where these canons of culture remain unmodified or are reinforced rather than reconstructed then we might assert that, for all the surface activity and turbulence in the system, the reality is that significant change has not occurred. This is clearly the case in relation to, for example, the curriculum 14–19 and to teaching and learning styles, and we explore this issue in Chapters 4 and 6. *Plus ça change, plus c'est la même chose.*

The second orthodoxy we wish to challenge emanates from our concern about the reality of change. It relates to the notion that there has been a steady and at times rapid growth in the value of vocational pathways through 14–19, and a concomitant decline in the emphasis on academic education, leading towards parity of esteem and integration between vocational and academic strands. While it is clear that this has been a strongly espoused political aim of successive governments, it is equally clear that this has not been achieved, and that the rhetoric reflects a political ideal of change that has insufficient force and momentum to overcome strong resistance to the notion across much of society. We consider this further in Chapter 5.

The third touchstone of the educational narrative is that there has been fundamental change in participation in learning and training amongst young people in the 16–19 age group, attributed by each of the key stakeholders in education (government and professionals) to their own vision, policy and practice. Concern about the low level of participation of young people post-16 has been a consistent theme of government policy since the late 1970s. Despite the actions to address this concern, by 2003 OECD data demonstrated that the UK is still only twenty-sixth out of 29 OECD countries in terms of participation in education and training at 17 – only Mexico, Greece and Turkey have lower participation rates. The drive to increase participation appears to have led to only relatively small increases in the numbers in education or training, but there is a shift in the pattern of what they do. Payne (2003) shows, using data from the England and Wales Youth Cohort Study (YCS), that in 1989 48 per cent of 16/17-year-olds were in full-time education, with 24 per cent in some form of workbase-related training and 23 per cent in full-time jobs. By 2002, 71 per cent were in full-time education, only 9 per cent in workbase-related training and 9 per cent in full-time employment. As Payne indicates, 'Thus the rise in participation in full-time education did not represent a sudden upsurge of interest in qualifications and skill development, but rather a shift in its location from the workplace to the classroom' (2003, p. 4).

Our fourth challenge is to the idea that the enhancement of choice for young people in relation to education and training will produce positive change within the system by ensuring the connection between the needs and wants of young people and the provision of education and training. Choice has impacted strongly on the culture of schools and colleges, and has certainly impacted on the relationships between institutions and organizations on the supply side of the market. However, it is not clear how far choice is a reality for most young people or whether the fundamental principles and tenets of education and training 14–19 have changed as a result of choice and marketization. Choice is inevitably constrained by a young person's context, and in reality for many young people choosing is what is done by the system, not by them – they are the objects not the purveyors of choice. And with choice comes personal demand. We shall explore elsewhere in this volume (Chapters 6 and 8) the stress and demand that choice can create for young people, and we shall show how the voice of young people is too rarely considered in the policy and practice of 14–19. Indeed, we should recognize that although there has been a strong rhetoric of young people's choice within the policy initiatives, the real concern of government has been to create a system that will feed the labour market to meet national economic aims. Markets and choice are just the means to this end rather than the end in themselves.

The changing scene that we have portrayed within this chapter indicates clearly that the 14–19 sector, despite three decades of frantic activity, may still have a long journey to travel to reach some of the goals identified for it in 1979 and again in 1997 when Thatcher and Blair respectively came to power. The notion of 14–19 as a coherent, connected and integrated phase of education and training has emerged only at the end of a long period of change and readjustment within those parts of the education business that fall within its ambit. As an idea, it has emerged strongly as a vision for the future, yet it is a highly contested concept that is by no means assured of success and acceptance, and is certainly a long way from realization. As such it represents but one more example of the conflict, contradiction, confusion and contestation that has characterized education and training policy and practice post-14 over the last quarter century in England.

Chapter 3

Moving the pieces around: structural change since 1979

Repositioning the elements

Chapter 2 argued that throughout the period from 1979, but particularly during a central period from 1988 to the end of the twentieth century, structural change was a key tactic of the government to bring about reform in the education and training system. The chapter also suggested that despite much rhetoric to the contrary, fundamentals have changed little. This chapter will explore the structural changes that were implemented in more detail, and the intended and unintended effects. Structure here is defined as 'the ordering of physical and symbolic elements of resources and experience into persistent patterns' (Lumby et al., 2003b). Defined in this way, structural change equates to transformations which involve adjustments to processes and culture, as well as the formal ordering of organizations. Other chapters deal with changes in process, for example, the fundamental process of teaching and learning. This chapter focuses primarily on physical elements of structure such as staff, the way relationships both within and between organizations are ordered, the way they are controlled and the cultural prescriptions about what is acceptable or proper in the way organizations are constituted.

Structure, of course, exists at a variety of levels. There is, first, the site of learning itself, the school, college or work-based learning company. Then there are local or regional bodies which contribute to the shaping of educational and training organizations, either directly as in the case of LEAs, or through the funds they disburse. Finally, there are national bodies, including government, which set overall parameters for the nature of education and training organizations and their activities. The exact division of control amongst these levels is subject to much debate. The locus of control, and the changing perception of where control may lie is a part of the pattern of structural change. Control is exerted to shape the nature of education and training organizations and the relations between them, overtly through the levers of legislation and resource. More subtly, control may be exerted through consumer choice and through internal micropolitical and external political forces. In effect, this chapter considers the motivation and strategy of the chess player, or more correctly, the chess players, the way that pieces have been moved around the board, and whether this has resulted in a win, lose or stalemate, and for whom.

The locus of control

Chapter 2 referred to the debate which followed Callaghan's Ruskin speech and the breakdown in the previous 'hands-off' approach to the control of education. Since that time there has been consistent experimentation with how to manage the system, reflecting not only the removal of power from professional educators, but also from local democracy, as the role of the local education authorities was eroded or, in the case of the incorporated post-16 sector from 1993, removed entirely.

From 1979 to the Education Reform Act in 1988, there was no concerted effort to challenge the control of education by the LEAs. A bolt-on in the form of the Manpower Services Commission was an initial experiment in how a national organization could offer funds and so shape training activity outside LEA control. However, from 1986, with the Conservative Party announcement of a new type of school, the city technology college, initiative after initiative followed which removed control from LEAs or bypassed them. Local Management of Schools offered the mass of schools a degree of autonomy to manage their own budgets. City technology colleges, grant maintained schools and specialist schools, have gone further and attempted to lure schools away from the bosom of LEAs by the double enticement of autonomy and additional funds. The LEAs have been retained as a go-between for the majority of schools, distributing national funding through the Standard Spending Assessment given to each authority. While the LEAs retain some discretion over spending, government has powers which can be invoked to prevent expenditure which it considers inappropriate. In this way, the power of LEAs to manage schools has been seriously weakened.

Colleges were offered the same inducements of autonomy and the possibility of more funds, though without any choice. However, the freedom from local authority control and the possibility of expanding and increasing funds through growth was generally welcomed in the further education sector. One principal described the majority of the sector as smiling while leaping off the cliff (Perry, 1997). A number of additional organizations were created to take over the role of distributing funds previously held by the LEAs, such as Training and Enterprise Councils, and from 2001, to co-ordinate provision. In defining and influencing appointment to the boards of the these organizations, government could attempt to influence the nature of the learning and teaching experience of 14–19-year-olds. Following the model of the Manpower Services Commission, which offered funds for education and training additional to and outside the control of the LEAs, quangos, at national level the Further Education Funding Council, since 2001 replaced by the Learning and Skills Council, and at local level Training and Enterprise Councils, replaced by Local Learning and Skills Councils (LLSCs), have had control of the purse strings and so, to some degree, the strategic plans of colleges and work-based learning providers. Funding was made available to be paid directly not only to state supported colleges, but also to private providers who offered training, and were therefore in competition with colleges, opening up the sector to competition with private trainers.

As well as core funding distributed through the LSC or the LEA, increasingly, funds are accessed through ring-fenced funding pools which are sourced directly from government and, though they may be administered by agencies and quangos, are directly shaped by government rules. The effects of the amount and method of distribution of resource have been a key lever for change and are considered more fully in Chapter 9.

Where, then, in the structure does control of 14–19 education and training lie? Research has inevitably uncovered conflicting or ambivalent accounts. For example, in the early post-incorporation years, principals complained both about the limitations on what they could do, established through legislation and through rulings from the Further Education Funding Council, but also complained that the FEFC did not exert control at all, in terms of co-ordinating and assuring provision (Lumby, 2001b). Those regretting the increasing involvement of government in education and training have been met with the argument that the consumer has the power and influence through increased choice and the decision to enrol in any particular institution or not. The quasi-market, not government, rules (Le Grand, 1990).

Noble and Pym (1989, pp. 32–3) advance a theory of the 'receding locus of power' in relation to complex organizations, where 'whatever the level one applies to the organization, the "real" decisions always seem to be taken somewhere else'. This theory may apply equally to the whole education and training system. Government would argue that they have devolved funds and powers to schools and colleges, and that decisions about strategy, and therefore control of destiny, lie with each organization's governing body. Schools and colleges may argue that given the restrictions on their core business, teaching and learning, through control of the National Curriculum and the National Qualifications Framework, and through the prescription of their actions by legislation and the availability and method of distribution of funds, they have little power. The intercessors in the form of LEAs and quangos, equally might argue they are prescribed in the influence they can exert by imposed government targets and regulations and the use that can be made of the funds they 'control'. At organizational level, Gleeson and Shain (1999) argue that power has shifted from professional educators to managers. Players at all levels appear to see the locus of control as moving from themselves to elsewhere.

Noble and Pym (1989, p. 33) provide a compelling description of the process of decision-making as 'hemmed in by decisions already taken elsewhere'. Thus at organizational level, teachers and lecturers see power and control shifting to senior leadership, particularly principals in chief executive mode and their senior leadership teams. At local and regional level, the locus of power would be perceived as lying with national government. The latter would, however, point to devolved regional and local powers, for example to LLSCs who can reshape local post-16 provision and to LEAs who may still open or close schools. In this way power flows around a cycle, each level seeing power at the next hierarchical level up and beyond, while the final level in the hierarchy, national government, sees the power being pushed down the system to the consumer, the providers and local or regional bodies, some of which remain democratic.

Morgan (1986) argues that power is conceived in a number of different ways, both as a resource to be used to gain control and as a relation between people and groups. Its sources are multiple, including:

1. formal authority
2. control of scarce resources
3. use of organizational structure, rules and regulations

4. control of decision processes
5. control of knowledge and information
6. control of boundaries
7. ability to cope with uncertainty
8. control of technology
9. interpersonal alliances, networks and control of 'informal organizations'
10. control of counter organizations
11. symbolism and the management of meaning
12. gender and the management of gender relations
13. structural factors that define the stage of action
14. the power one already has (adapted from Morgan, 1986, p. 159).

Each of these sources is available and in use at multiple levels in education and training. For example, resource is controlled at national level, but also by the principal/head of each organization. Therefore, no individual educator or organization is in a position of absolute power, nor are they powerless. However, Morgan (1986, p. 185) makes it clear that power is 'a great deal to do with asymmetrical patterns of dependence'. Government has manipulated many of the sources of power in its own interests, resulting in a weight of advantage. Legislation is the ultimate means of formal authority. Control of scarce resources has increasingly been a tactic to increase power as government reduces the unit of resource for educating a learner. Decision-making processes are increasingly controlled by government through its imposition of frameworks and parameters, particularly to access funds. The demand for information by government has grown exponentially, with schools and colleges required to submit ever more detailed accounts of their activity. The technology of teaching and learning, formerly the province of professional educators, is increasingly prescribed through government-controlled departments and quangos. Morgan makes the point that the acquisition of power is cumulative. The more one has, the easier it is to gain. The process of government increasing its power reflects this, as it has gained momentum steadily since 1979. Finally, while it is clear that some power can be exerted even by the most lowly within the system, the exercise of power is constrained by the structures established by the most powerful. Thus, heads can only control scarce resources because government has legislated to allow them to do so. Though the location of powers to make specific decisions remains contested and, in Noble and Pym's terms, may appear to recede to those in the system, increasingly, the system is structured to create ever greater dependence on government and to locate power with government.

Elements of structure

People

One of the drivers of change of 14–19 education and training has been the desire to increase the numbers of young people not absenting themselves but achieving in school up to 16, and remaining in the system beyond 16 (Hodgson and Spours, 2003). This aim has clear cost implications. Successive governments, however, have sought the means to meet the resource requirements without proportionate rises in expenditure. Given that anything from 70 to 90 per cent of the budget of education and training organizations is dedicated to staff costs, inevitably one of the means of change in the input:output ratio for education is adjusting the structure of the workforce. Both schools and colleges have been subject to such change with modifications in the profile of those supporting learning away from professionally qualified educators only, to a more mixed body of staff who may include a larger proportion of those who have lesser qualifications than teachers, or qualifications deriving from professional bodies rather than academic disciplines.

'Remodelling the workforce' has been couched by government in relation to schools in very positive terms, as advantaging teachers and being driven by a desire to release them from tasks inappropriate to their skills and training:

> Remodelling is about giving teachers more time, extra support and renewed leadership. This is essential if they are to go on improving standards in schools. By restructuring the teaching profession and reforming the school workforce, we can reduce teacher workload, raise standards, increase job satisfaction and improve the status of the profession. (DFES, 2003d)

Despite the emphasis on relieving teachers of only inappropriate tasks, it is clear that support staff will be undertaking core tasks which were previously undertaken by teachers. A survey of over 1,200 teaching assistants discovered that: '50% of the teaching assistants deliver lessons prepared by a teacher, 80% mark pupils' work and 46% contribute to lesson planning' (GMB, 2003, p. 2).

While teachers sometimes feel threatened by the advent of, as they see it, lesser qualified and lesser paid staff as a substitute for themselves, teaching assistants feel that the value of their role is underplayed and that it is being developed to suit the interests of teachers and/or government, rather than themselves or, critically, learners. The survey found that: 'Respondents feel that their status within schools is generally low, reflected in lack of understanding and consistency when it comes to job titles and roles. Many feel they are treated as "second class", "invisible", "spare parts" or "servants"' (GMB, 2003, p. 2). Only 38 per cent were included in staff meetings. Furthermore, the survey discovered nearly half of the teaching assistants were on fixed-term or temporary contracts. If, increasingly, support for learners is undertaken by those who are valued less than teachers, including by teachers and headteachers themselves (GMB, 2003), there are implications for the messages given to learners. Not only are learners commodified, but it seems that restructuring the workforce has resulted in a hierarchy of staff which commodifies certain sections of staff, as a disposable convenience to be paid during term time only, to be used to do the less interesting and unpalatable tasks and whose employment can be ended quickly and painlessly. As in so much else, the interests of learners are not centre stage. Instead, appeasing teachers through emphasizing the benefits to them, even at the cost of treating other staff in dubious ways, reflects the reality of power relations, as those with least power, support staff and learners, receive less consideration.

The workforce remodelling in the Learning and Skills sector has followed similar lines but has been more overt in its link with cost reduction and in securing for employers the advantages of a less expensive and more flexible workforce. Since 1993 over a fifth of the workforce has been made redundant. Of those remaining, there has been a 30 per cent turnover of lecturing and senior staff and 32 per cent of principals have left their post (Gleeson, 2001; Shain, 1999). The renegotiation of the contract terms of lecturers which followed 1993 through the replacement of the 'Silver Book' terms, resulted in lecturers teaching more hours, with fewer holidays (Hewitt and Crawford, 1997). There was an increase in the range of duties for all, so that administrative and management duties previously undertaken by heads of department with several hours remission from teaching were now distributed amongst a range of 'team leaders' and lecturers (Baldwin, 2003; Goulding et al., 1998). In England by 1995, over half of staff were on part-time contracts (FEDA, 1995). Agency staff, who earned less, had fewer rights and were temporary, worked alongside permanent staff. Additionally, large numbers of administrative staff and managers from outside the education field were recruited, both at senior levels as managers of estates, finance and personnel, and lower down the system as student counsellors, information and communications technology (ICT) specialists and so on. Overall the workforce has changed considerably, with a much wider range of roles, including those supporting learning. The mapping of the FE sector (FEDA, 1995) identified 45 different job titles for those who support learning outside the formal lecturing/teaching role. Goulding et al. (1998) noted that two-thirds of colleges in their survey had introduced such posts and that most planned to increase their number, in order to increase flexibility, to focus more on learning rather than teaching, to contain staffing costs and to free teaching staff from non-essential duties.

There are undoubtedly advantages to this reformation of the workforce, in offering flexibility and a wide range of expertise. Nevertheless, the movement from a largely education-trained workforce to a wider range of backgrounds, from full-time permanent to an assortment of temporary arrangements, from a majority of lecturers with relatively fewer administrative and management staff to a much lower ratio of academic to support staff, amounts to a structural change in the workforce which is driven by more than just pedagogic justification.

The shift echoes similar changes in other parts of the world. In the vocational education and training sector in Australia, full-time male employment has declined while the proportion of women and of part-time staff has grown sharply (Shah, 2003). This pattern is also evident in North America, where the number of part-time faculty (academic staff) in community colleges had grown to 65 per cent by 1995 from a base of 41 per cent in 1973 (Levin, 2001). Levin also notes the frequent restructuring of the college workforce, with administrative processes streamlined, at least in intention, and the removal of posts. In a survey of English further education colleges undertaken in 1999, restructuring was indicated as the most significant tool adopted to achieve cultural change for the period 1993–99. Of the 164 colleges responding, only four had not restructured. The majority had restructured more than once and 10 per cent had restructured over three times. Thus, the experience of ongoing change in the number, role and contract of staff employed in further education, and the relationship between them as evidenced by organizational structures, appears to be spread throughout the world, suggesting that workforce changes are a response to global rather than merely UK forces. Exogenous economically and socially derived pressure to increase participation, and raise levels of achievement, allied to the political decision not to raise expenditure proportionately have translated into structural change at regional, local and organizational level. In all cases, initiators would argue that the fundamental drivers were rational aims of improving teaching and learning and becoming more cost-efficient. However, on some more fundamental plane, players at all four levels, national, regional, local and organizational, have embraced change resulting in a shift in cultural assumptions about who should support learners and the relationship between different roles, amounting to what Levin (2001) characterizes as a paradigm shift.

While the changes have been most apparent in post-16 education in FE colleges, the advent of more flexible arrangements to support 14–16-year-olds, particularly Pathfinder Partnership projects, has seen a leaching into schools of the more varied workforce arrangements established in the further education sector. Connexions advisers, student counsellors and detached youth workers are all examples of the growth of roles to support young people in schools in the 14–19 age range, beyond formal teaching staff. Nevertheless, changes have been relatively slight compared with those in the Learning and Skills sector and also compared to early years provision, where a wholesale reform has taken place, reconstituting work teams drawing from education, social services and health professionals. In this way secondary schools are sandwiched between parts of the education and training system where the remodelling of the workforce has been much more dramatic. The signs remain that, though proceeding cautiously, a wider range of roles both to support learning, such as higher-level teaching assistants, and to support business services, such as bursars, are increasing. The demand for staff with different skills and qualifications is also growing as schools appoint those able to offer vocational education and training rather than traditional academic programmes.

Organizational structure and diversity

Alongside the changes in the people employed, there has been an extended period of apparent change in the nature of the organizations themselves. There has been an attempt to change the structure in terms of the types of school and college, and the relations between them. Experimentation has been embedded in the strategy of encouraging 'diversity'. The overt rationale has been the encouragement of school specialisms of various kinds, in order to offer more choice to the consumer, whether conceived as the parent or learner. The vision of a local range of providers, each offering a distinctive curriculum, has in fact not quite played out in this way. Edwards and Whitty (1997) review the advent of city technology colleges (CTCs), grant maintained (GM) schools and specialist schools and conclude that there is no evidence that parents and learners are choosing a particular school on the basis of its curriculum. In CTCs, for example, the links with industry and above average ICT provision were not the attractor. Rather, in the case of CTCs, and many specialist schools, it is the option of partial selection, and the related belief that this secures a traditional academic curriculum which is the lodestone to parents and children. Religious schools and specialist schools both appear to be able to manipulate the criteria for selecting against aptitude, interest or religion, to enable them to secure a more academically able intake than other comprehensive schools (Gorard and Taylor, 2001).

In summary, the conclusions of a variety of research into the effect of initiatives to increase choice and diversity and thereby raise participation and achievement are:

- Many choosers look for schools where there is some degree of selection and a traditional academic curriculum. They are not generally interested in other specializations in the curriculum (Glatter et al., 1997).
- Competition has encouraged similarity rather than differences in the curriculum of schools (Edwards and Whitty, 1997).
- Rather than securing better life chances for children from disadvantaged backgrounds, diverse schools have tended to increase social reproduction (Gewirtz et al., 1995).

Overall, the encouragement of 'diversity' has in fact embedded further market predilections for achieving entry to a school as like a traditional grammar school as is feasible. Parents as well as children have subjected themselves to scrutiny as to their family/child's suitability for entry to popular schools. While achievement in terms of value-added has risen amongst schools where there is a degree of specialism of some sort, the debate continues as to whether the rise is above that which would have been achieved in the authority had differentiated schools not existed, or whether the rise is at the cost of neighbouring schools, so there is no overall rise in achievement (Gorard and Taylor, 2001; Schagen and Schagen, 2003).

The same thrust to diversify is apparent to a lesser degree amongst colleges and work-based learning providers in the Learning and Skills sector. Colleges have always been differentiated to some degree. Sixth form colleges were established in the 1960s and numbers grew as part of the comprehensive reorganization of secondary education, often created from existing grammar schools. By 1992 there were 117 sixth form colleges catering for almost 25 per cent of the country's sixth form students (Shorter, 1994). They were administered by the LEAs quite separately to further education colleges. From their inception they were in competition with schools which retained their sixth forms and also with the independent sector. There were also approximately 300 further education colleges including specialist agricultural and horticultural and art and design colleges. From 1993, all were incorporated and received their funding from the Further Education Funding Council and from 2001, the Learning and Skills Councils. To some extent, therefore, although colleges were drawn away from the control of LEAs and amalgamated into one sector, no different options were created. The same institutions continued. However, a tactic similar to that in schools has crept in with the establishment of Centres of Vocational Excellence (COVEs) which rather like specialist schools, aim to offer a choice of curriculum which is particularly strong along one or more dimensions. The number of COVE centres is planned to be expanded, offering the option to attend a college with specialist strength.

14–19 provision

The motivation of government is no more easy to unravel than that of an individual. The reasons for change as discerned through policy statements and legislation are no more reliable than self-reported data from any source. At one level, rational arguments are presented for a course of action. At another level, the actions which follow may seem to indicate different or even contradictory drivers. For example, the stated aims of increasing equity, choice and autonomy within education are appraised though the fractured perspective of many players, each of whom may interpret change in a different way. Two areas only appear to be consistent intentions throughout the period; first, the shifting of control away from the local education authorities, apparently to more devolved and numerous centres, and secondly, a determined effort to 'massify' the system (Hodgson and Spours, 2003, p. 11) to engage more 14–19-year-olds in remaining in education or training until 19.

Where then, does 14–19 provision sit in the structural or apparent structural changes that have been reviewed in this chapter? While there are examples of 11–14 schools, such as in the Isle of Wight, the National Curriculum has encouraged some authorities with middle school structures where learners change to another school at 14, to revert to 11–16 or 11–18 structures. Consequently, choice at 14 is a non-event for most. Choice of school is made at 11, and it is rare for learners to change again prior to 16. Only with the advent of Pathfinder projects encouraging collaboration between schools and colleges to offer alternative provision for year 10 and 11 pupils, has choice beyond what is available in a school chosen at an earlier point, become formally a possibility. Structural change has impacted on 14–19-year-olds, but not generally through their having choice at 14 beyond subject options in their school. The latter have changed little, as choices at 11 and 16 have largely offered similar options to those which existed prior to 1979. Indeed, Pring argues that the list of subjects available within the National Curriculum 'is not dissimilar from that of the 1904 Regulations for secondary schools' (Pring, 1990, p. 70). The extent to which the curriculum has changed is dealt with more fully in Chapter 4.

Fourteen to nineteen education and training is still subject to the 11–16 and 16–19 structures, with two points in time with the potential for choice. At 11, despite the advent of various 'new' categories of school (CTCs, GM, specialist), the range of options is not very different to those that were available prior to 1979. The grant maintained option allowed some schools which would have closed to remain open, thus retaining existing choices. The growth of specialist and religious schools has facilitated the retention of schools which select on grounds other than primarily catchment area. For the majority, choices between providers have changed little. The process of accessing those choices has also remained stable in its nature. Entry to preferred schools relates to the social capital of the individual and their family. Those able to move house, offer academic ability or aptitude, or parents knowledgeable about and skilful in manipulating the system, find it easier to gain access to popular schools, and these are still largely identified using traditional criteria of selective intake and academic excellence. At 16, young people can still choose between a school sixth form, or a college within the Learning and Skills Sector, or work-based learning, amongst such options as exist within their locality. The structure has not changed fundamentally, nor have choices and the likelihood of accessing them.

The most compelling and influential structures are those of socio-economic class and culture, and it is these structures which persist and easily override or transmute initiatives apparently designed to erode inequities and create wider options. Even more, the initiatives which appear designed for such ends may, as in the case of the series of differentiated categories of school, disguise the further embedding of social inequalities (Woods and Levačić, 2002). For example, while overt moves to establish grammar schools have been politically unsafe, the covert retention of selection has found a channel through specialist or religious schools. Those who have gained advantage and power by the existing system have an intense motivation to further embed the underpinning values which have proved so successful in their case (Reay, 2001a). As Ball (2003) describes it, education has been and remains a war zone between groups with privilege and those without.

Hodgson and Spours (2003) characterize the period from 1976 to 1986 as dominated by curriculum change with an emphasis on 'new vocationalism'. This period indeed had little structural change other than bolted on elements such as the Manpower Services Commission running schemes largely targeted at the 16–19 young unemployed. From the late 1980s throughout the 1990s there appears to have been much more concerted effort at structural change within the system. The erosion or removal of LEA management and the creation of additional controlling quangos apparently changed the locus of power. The increased autonomy given to schools and colleges through their governing bodies and the reshaping of the workforce were presented as means to reform the responsiveness and quality of providers. At all levels constant reorganization has led to a belief that change has occurred (Fullan, 2003). However, neither the learning experience, nor the equity within the system appear to have shifted. In a series of seminars facilitated by the Nuffield Foundation, Raffe laments the persistence of issues which were debated in relation to 14–19-year-olds in the 1980s and 1990s:

The poor motivation and attitudes of young people; inadequate participation in education and training; the poor labour-market incentives to learn; the weaknesses of vocational pathways and the marginal position of work based learning; the barriers imposed by a divided and age related qualifications system; poor quality and low attainment. (Raffe, 2002, p. 9)

Reality check

Given this picture, the structural changes explored in the chapter can be understood most easily as *ritual* designed to achieve what Galbraith (1983, p. 5) characterized as 'conditioned power', that is, a process of persuading or enrolling people in submission to a way of doing things, but without their conscious awareness of the process of submission. Lutz (1988) argues for a parallel between pre-literate society's use of witch-finding and processes in education. Where the causes of failure in society are unclear, and some disaster threatens or strikes, in the absence of a rational response, a 'witch' is sought to blame, is eliminated or punished, and the status quo thus restored.

Successive governments have been unable accurately to locate the causes of the relatively poor educational performance of the UK compared to other economically developed nations. Consequently, to some degree, LEAs and teachers/lecturers have served as 'witches' and have been punished, eliminated or weakened. It would seem that the reorganization of elements of the education system since 1979 have, first, fragmented and confused. The locus of control has become contested and unclear. Secondly, the changes in the control system, the workforce profile and the curriculum offering which defines each education and training organization have served only to further embed the values and social class differentials which pre-existed. Government has conducted elaborate rites, in which scapegoats such as LEAs and teachers have been identified, but the changes ultimately confirm the status quo.

PART 2

A COHERENT LEARNING EXPERIENCE?

Chapter 4

Curriculum 14–19: parallel worlds or brave new world?

Of the three waves of policy characterizing 14–19 since 1979, the one which has had the most direct impact on the lives of young people has been curriculum change. Yet, despite its centrality to their lives, the curriculum is something imposed upon young people rather than negotiated with them, characterizing the power relationships in the 14–19 sector. It forms, therefore, part of the ritual of educating and socializing young people in ways reflecting the ideologies and cultural values of key stakeholders in society. This chapter explores curriculum change in more detail, and identifies how far the vision, aims and objectives enshrined in each key curriculum innovation have been achieved.

The roots of curriculum

So what should young people learn and experience between 14 and 19? What opportunities should be available to them? What can we reasonably expect 19-year-olds to have achieved? Are there aspects of learning which *all* young people should experience, irrespective of their intended destination? How much choice should the curriculum provide? The 14–19 curriculum is, more than any other, fraught with fundamental questions that have strong political, ideological and philosophical dimensions, and the curriculum will reflect the purpose of education that its designers wish to achieve (Ahier and Ross, 1995). Scrimshaw (1983) has described five main philosophical perspectives on education:

1. Classical humanism, reflecting the philosophy of Plato and the view that education should meet the broad needs of society, with individuals educated in the way that reflects their place in a hierarchical society.

2. Liberal humanism, reflecting the views of Rousseau, that education seeks to help individuals achieve personal and moral development for the benefit of society.

3. Progressivism, associated with Dewey, where the purpose of education is to produce individuals who can think for themselves and be active participants in a democratic society

4. Instrumentalism, which sees education as serving the economic needs of the state, with individuals trained to perform their roles within the workforce.

5. Reconstructionism, which sees education as the mechanism for implementing social change, often in pursuit of particular ideologies.

Education in England has traditionally emphasized a classical humanist view, based on academic education for those who will be the leaders and key players within society, and a vocational route involving employment and technical training for the rest. The English education system during the 1960s and 1970s had a short flirtation with progressivism, through pupil-centred approaches to primary education and the establishment of a comprehensive school system. The turbulence in the wake of the Great Debate, though, saw the strong imposition of instrumentalism, and the 14–19 sector became a philosophical battle between those espousing classical humanist perspectives and those pursuing instrumentalist objectives. We explore the main battlefields below.

The 14–16 experience

Our first battlefield is the curriculum for 14–16-year-olds (Key Stage 4 of the National Curriculum since 1990). In 1979 the curriculum distinguished between General Certificate of Education Ordinary level (O level) examinations aimed at the top 20 per cent of the ability range, and the Certificate of Secondary Education aimed at the next 40 per cent. Both were essentially academic in character, with assessment designed to test knowledge and understanding in relation to traditional subjects. However, increasing dissatisfaction with this system emanated from two concerns. First, the existence of two examination systems was educationally and socially divisive, particularly since their roots lay in different school traditions. Secondly, the emphasis on testing through written examinations was seen to reward rote learning and a narrow range of skills. The recognition that the assessment methods narrowed the achievement possibilities for most pupils suggested that a reform of the curriculum and assessment methods was needed.

The chosen solution was GCSE, a curriculum with clear learning objectives identifying the knowledge, understanding and skills that would be tested, and assessment based on enabling pupils to demonstrate positive achievement, that is, to enable them to show what they 'know, understand and can do'. This stood in contrast to O levels and CSEs which had been criticized as offering a deficit approach to testing in which the aim was to establish what pupils did not know. This was to be achieved by adopting a criterion-referenced assessment system rather than the norm-referenced approach of O level/CSE, and widening the range of assessment methods. Since 1988 GCSE has remained as the benchmark 'school-leaver' examination, and this unified system has become one of the key mechanisms for judging not only the performance of individual pupils, but also that of the schools themselves. Its primacy, however, has not meant that its history has been free from issues and debates.

First, as we identified in Chapter 2, GCSE provides a curriculum strongly rooted in the academic tradition of the grammar school, and connects most strongly with academic programmes post-16, such as A level, rather than with the vocational or training programmes that many young people enter. Linked to this is the concern that GCSE has done little to reduce the disenchantment with the school curriculum of those in the lower half of the attainment profile.

Secondly, the removal of the notion of pass/fail in favour of a grade system running from A to G has not prevented the use of the achievement of the higher grades (Grade C and above) as being deemed the 'pass' standard both by schools and within the wider community. Cockett and Callaghan (1996, p. 56) describe the existence of the 'Grade C cliff' as indicative of the political and social importance of this boundary, and the persistence of the use of a 16+ examination as a selection device. Hence the ritual of selection at 16 has been retained, and the manipulation of the achievement data in school league tables has created clear sub-groups – those with five or more GCSEs at Grade C or better; those with one to four GCSEs at Grade C or better; those with no GCSEs at Grade C or better; and those with no GCSEs at any grade. The post-16 fate of these groups is little different than those who in the 1970s would have been sorted as: five or more O level passes; one to four O level passes; CSE passes at grades less than Grade 1; and those with no CSE awards.

Thirdly, the shift in assessment methods has raised concerns about the impact on a number of sub-groups, and also on the comparability of achievement levels with those of two decades earlier. While levels of pupil achievement have risen steadily since 1988, with the numbers obtaining five or more Grade Cs (or better) rising from 43 per cent to over 50 per cent, this improvement has been mainly the result of increasing achievement by girls, so that there is now a marked difference between girls' achievement and boys' achievement (a reversal of the situation under the O level/CSE system). This is attributable to many positive dimensions of GCSE. The testing of a wider range of attributes, for example, gives individuals the opportunity to genuinely demonstrate positive achievement. This, too, is aided by increasing skill amongst the teaching force to prepare students for assessment. A negative interpretation of the improvement, however, attributes the changes to the 'dumbing down' of the assessment methods and required standards, and the possibility of undue assistance from teachers and parents in the preparation of coursework assessment material.

The introduction of GCSE only shortly pre-dated the introduction of a highly prescriptive National Curriculum (NC) over the period 1988–91. This centralized control of the curriculum and a strong underpinning system of accountability measured through national tests provided the zenith of national centralized curriculum control. With assessment at the end of Key Stage 3 (at age 14) as a baseline for each pupil, it became possible to measure both individual and school progression for pupils over Key Stage 4. The intended model was never formally put in place, however, in that compulsion across the whole 10-subject curriculum in Key Stage 4 was rescinded before any pupils completed it. Short courses (rather than full GCSEs) were made available in many subjects (for example, in Humanities) for those pupils choosing to specialize in other aspects of the curriculum, and schools were permitted to disapply the NC requirements in relation to Modern Languages in Key Stage 4 from 1992.

After 1995 this retreat from GCSE accelerated for the lowest quartile in the cohort achievement profile. First, disapplication enabled schools to consider alternative programmes for them. This resulted in the broadening of the curriculum to include vocational, pre-vocational and skills based programmes. Foundation level GNVQs, for example, provided a vocationally focused programme in areas such as 'Business', and included direct experience of work environments and work-related skills, with the final award being deemed equivalent to GCSE in level. Other awards, for exam-

ple, the ASDAN awards, gave opportunities for pupils to pursue programmes with a wide range of skills and social context underpinning their
organization. From 1998 FE colleges were permitted to allow pupils under
16 to take programmes in college. This work-related curriculum has
expanded significantly so that by 2003 40 per cent of 16-year-olds include
some work-related learning within their programme over and above the 95
per cent who undertake brief work experience (Raffo, 2003). The White
Paper *21st Century Skills: Realising our Potential* (DfES, 2003e) seeks to ensure
such work-related learning is available to all pupils in the 14–16 age range.
In addition, the pull of the academic curriculum is strong and, in 2001–03,
GCSE programmes in vocational subjects such as engineering were introduced. Their success reflects their appeal in terms of content and subject
matter with pupils who had begun to opt for vocational programmes,
combined with the academic credibility to parents, schools and employers
of their currency in GCSE terms. Hence the vocational thrust was pulled
back by the power of the academic, and the contradictions and confusion
of the 14–16 curriculum have been reasserted.

The curriculum model that underpins the final years of compulsory
schooling is rooted in a classical humanist tradition focused through an
instrumentalist and centralizing political lens. The 14-year-old in 2004 is
faced with a similar choice to that of his or her parents, except that those
not wishing to engage with the academic curriculum have a more formal
set of other pathways to engage them. Despite a quarter century of
changes, the fundamental structure and nature of the 14–16 curriculum
remains the same.

The vocational curriculum post-16

The second of our curriculum battlefields is the post-16 vocational arena.
Beyond 18 the majority of the age cohort is to be found in employment
rather than in formal education, although the age at which they enter the
labour market has, on average, risen since 1979. In 1979, for the majority
of 16-year-olds, and certainly all of those in the bottom two attainment
quartiles, their 16–19 'curriculum' was based firmly in the workplace, and
mostly with little or no training. Where training was part of the experience
it was delivered either formally through traditional apprenticeships, which
included 'day release' training at local FE colleges, or through other training
provided by FE in response to the demands of local industry or the 24

Industry Training Boards, established in 1964. Dissatisfaction with this model was widespread amongst both employers and participants, and two issues were identified as in need of addressing – the lack of a single national integrated framework of vocational training, and the lack of provision for those entering semi-skilled and unskilled jobs, who represented the majority of the school leaver cohort.

The spectre of rising youth unemployment prompted the emergence, in succession, of two key training schemes – the Youth Opportunities Programme, which operated from 1978 to 1983, and the Youth Training Scheme, introduced in 1983 and replaced in 1989 by Youth Training. The YOP was designed 'to provide unemployed young people under the age of 19 with training and work experience appropriate to their individual needs and to help each individual secure a permanent job at the earliest possible opportunity' (Farley, 1985, p. 78). It provided training for 200,000 young people each year, but rapidly fell into low public repute because of criticisms that:

1. Unemployment rates for YOP leavers remained high.
2. The nature of the training provided was often limited and inade-quate.
3. Employers were using the scheme for job substitution rather than for training.
4. There was a lack of equality of opportunity, particularly for Asian and Afro-Caribbean ethnic groups.

The YTS was introduced to address these issues but, despite its better connection between employers and the MSC in terms of quality assurance, curriculum design and administration, the standing criticisms relating to YOP largely remained.

In parallel to the experiments of the YOP and the YTS, termed 'new vocationalism', ran the evolution of employment-based training routes that had their origin in traditional models of apprenticeship. The wide diversity of vocational training reflected the independent evolution of training in each main occupational field, and presented an inchoate picture. As Cantor et al. (1995, p. 48) indicate, 'the diversity of aims of the courses … and the variety of objectives of those studying them have presented substantial obstacles to those who have tried to create study experiences which have common elements for students throughout the sector'. The curriculum in these fields was provided by some 200 examining and validating bodies, the largest of which were the Business and Technology Education Council BTEC), the Royal Society of Arts (RSA) and City and Guilds (C&G), but which included many occupationally specific bodies such as the Construction Industry Training Board.

To provide a comprehensive model of training, government established in 1986 the National Council for Vocational Qualifications to draw up a national training framework model. The NCVQ existed as a separate body until merging with the School Curriculum and Assessment Authority in 1997 to form the Qualifications and Curriculum Authority, and was throughout its existence a battlefield of curriculum philosophy. Its major success was the establishment of a national qualifications framework, built around a five-level model, which still provides the basis for all qualifications nationally, both academic and vocational.

This success, however, was frequently overshadowed by the continuing challenge of seeking to clarify, rationalize and co-ordinate the diverse vocational curricula that existed (Raggett, 1994). The NCVQ, under the strong influence of Gilbert Jessup (Jessup, 1991), initially set out to ensure that vocational training was based on curricula that, while they covered essential knowledge and understanding, were assessed through performance measures or competences. While few argued against the notion of skills-focused training, an entirely competence-based model raised two concerns. The first was that most existing curricula combined knowledge, understanding and skills elements to varying degrees, and therefore used a variety of assessment methods both in the workplace and in the examination room. Hence a change to a solely competence-based model would be challenging for many examination bodies. Secondly, the notion of competence-based learning was subject to significant criticism itself, well summarized by Burke (1995) and Armitage et al. (1999):

1. 'Competence' is incapable of subtle differentiation. An individual is either competent at a particular skill, or not, and there is no spectrum of achievement to distinguish the excellent from the 'merely competent'.

2. Competence-based models value only performance dimensions of learning, which are easily demonstrable. However, the essence of professional skill is the integration of that element of learning with knowledge and understanding, which is hard to assess in competency-based models (Wolf and Black, 1990).

3. Assessment of competency is innately challenging and is based on

subjective rather than objective judgements. This leads to variability of judgement, and hence there is a need for a complex system of verification to seek to ensure consistency of standards.

4. Competency-based models make learning assessment-led, with students and teachers focusing on those aspects of learning which are measurable at the expense of those (often higher order) aspects of learning which are not.

5. Competency-based approaches are not concerned about the process of learning, only with outcomes.

6. By pre-specifying outcomes, flexibility and spontaneity are inhibited, which can lead to a narrow and impoverished curriculum.

7. The pre-specification of outcomes limits and deprofessionalizes the role of the teacher.

As a result of these concerns the NCVQ became rather more flexible in the constraints it placed on curriculum design. Assessment through formal written tests was permitted, as was assessment other than in the workplace. By the time the NCVQ merged into the QCA most vocational training had, therefore, come into the NVQ framework and, as a result, some rationalization of examination and validation bodies occurred – by 1996 there were a mere 130 different bodies operating in this field!

The failures of the YOP and the YTS moved the emphasis from seeking to deal with employment problems *after* they had occurred to addressing fundamental issues of employability for young people *before* they enter the labour market (Ainley, 1990; Willis, 1987). This view saw a shift of vocational training from training environments (for example, the workplace) to educational environments (that is, the classroom) – a shift that Armitage et al. (1999) have characterized as from 'training for jobs' to 'training without jobs' (in the 1980s) to 'education without jobs' (from 1990 onwards). This in turn represents a shifting balance away from occupationally specific training to general vocational education in the 16–19 curriculum.

Early developments reflected the views of the Further Education Unit's report *A Basis for Choice* (FEU, 1979) and led to the establishment of, first, the abortive Certificate of Extended Education (CEE), which was essentially a further academic programme, and then, from 1984, the Certificate of Pre-Vocational Education (CPVE). The CPVE sought to 'continue general education within the context of vocational study as a preparation for adult and working life' (Cantor et al., 1995, p. 56).

Much more significant, though, was the introduction of General

National Vocational Qualifications. Suggested in the White Paper *Education and Training for the 21st Century* (DES/DE, 1991), they emerged as an attempt to broaden the curriculum available for full-time post-16 students. Specifically they were intended to provide a bridge between academic and vocational programmes, to equip young people with the skills and understanding required on entry to employment. Focused on key occupational areas (for example, Business, Health and Social Care) they had at their core:

- the development of key occupational knowledge and understanding
- a competence-based approach to assessment
- an individual, learner-centred approach to the curriculum
- the integration of key skills.

The GNVQ evolved rapidly during the 1990s, so that by 1999 some 25 per cent of 16–19-year-old full-time students were taking GNVQ awards (Hodgson-Wilson, 2004; Hodkinson, 1998). Significant adjustments to the detailed curriculum content and the balance of different assessment methods meant that its development and integration into the 16–19 curriculum was hugely demanding of time for schools and colleges. Despite criticism of the relatively high failure rate for students on GNVQ programmes and of the overly bureaucratic assessment systems (Bates, 2002; Bloomer, 1998), in essence, the GNVQ reflects a successful curriculum innovation that met the needs of the broader full-time 16–19 population, and its success underlay its full integration into Curriculum 2000, albeit in modified format (see below).

A third development was the growth and integration of core/key skills during the 1990s (Bolton and Hyland, 2003). An important criticism of both traditional academic curricula and of YTS/YOP programmes was their poor development of skills appropriate to the world of work, an issue highlighted by the Confederation of British Industry (CBI) report *Towards a Skills Revolution* (CBI, 1989). In February 1989 Kenneth Baker (Secretary of State for Education) suggested in a speech to the Association of Colleges that core skills should be a compulsory part of the post-16 curriculum, and the subsequent National Curriculum Council report (NCC, 1990) recommended the integration of skills in relation to communication, problem-solving, personal skills, numeracy, information technology and modern languages. The evolution of the GNVQ after 1992 saw the integration of key skills (known here as core skills) into the specifications, but with a focus only on literacy, numeracy and IT. Following the Dearing review (Dearing, 1996) their inclusion within A level programmes developed, using a similarly narrow definition of core skills. Despite the emphasis on the importance of skills development, however, the reality of their place within the 16–19 curriculum is that they have been adopted in a rather half-hearted way (Hodgson and Spours, 2002).

One other front in the battle of new vocationalism illustrates well the pursuit of change but the limits to progress – the reconfiguration of vocational training through the establishment of Modern Apprenticeships (MAs). The introduction of MAs reflected a concern about the declining number of young people following traditional apprenticeships, and the absence of apprenticeships in many occupational sectors. Modern apprenticeships were introduced in 1995 to provide specific vocational education and training leading to awards at Level 3 within the NVQ framework (that is, equivalent to A level). They were established in collaboration with the sector-specific national training organizations (NTOs), and funded and managed through local TECs (later, local LSCs). The numbers of young people undertaking MAs has grown steadily since their inception, although uptake and completion rates have varied substantially both geographically and between occupational sectors. Overall, though, they are not valued highly as an alternative to an academic pathway, are little understood, even by careers advisers in schools, and have been frequently readjusted and reorganized to advance their profile. Through this process they have contributed substantially to the curriculum confusion facing many young people and have not significantly advanced the rhetoric of the promotion of vocational pathways (Foskett and Hemsley-Brown, 1999).

The post-16 academic curriculum

The provision of a specialized academic curriculum for 16–19-year-olds is a distinctive feature of the education system in England. Designed to provide a pathway to university to follow the short, intense British undergraduate programmes, the A level has been frequently described as 'the gold standard' of the education system. Almost from its introduction in 1951, however, the A level was subjected to important criticisms:

1. The breadth of curriculum it provides is narrow and specialized.
2. Its focus is entirely academic with no attention to wider vocational needs.
3. A level syllabuses emphasize knowledge and understanding, with little attention to skills, either subject specific or generic.

4. Syllabuses are designed to meet the needs of higher education rather than the needs of 16–19-year-olds.

5. The A level was designed for the top 10 per cent in achievement terms, and has become anachronistic as the proportion of young people participating in 16–19 education has grown substantially.

Attempts to reform the A level have been strongly resisted by government, even when their own concerns had stimulated formal review of the system (Higham et al., 1996). The political imperative of meeting the perception of the A level as the gold standard in the eyes of middle-class voters has always caused government to step back from the path of reform, and the system has frequently seen the ritual of reviewing the A level then rejecting alternatives. The Higginson Committee (DES, 1988), for example, proposed the introduction of a five-subject A level, and there have been frequent calls for a British baccalaureate (Hodgson and Spours, 1997: IPPR,1990), yet the traditional A level model has remained largely untouched, with only 25 per cent including even GNVQ courses within their programmes.

Curriculum 2000 – the end of the war?

We have considered the post-16 curriculum so far in terms of the two dimensions of the academic–vocational divide. Despite the rhetoric of integration and 'parity of esteem' the curriculum adjustments of the previous quarter century still left a divided and unintegrated education and training system by 1997. The government's consultation paper *Qualifying for Success* (DfEE, 1997b) emphasized the concern about the 'triple track' model (training, NVQs, MAs; GNVQs; A levels) in the 16–19 sector and set out a programme of restructuring to address those concerns. Despite the opportunity for radical change, the model that emerged, later to be called Curriculum 2000, retained the centrality of A level, committed to the retention of an adjusted Advanced GNVQ as the Advanced Vocational Certificate of Education (AVCE) (as recommended by the Dearing review) and sought change through emphasizing the connections and comparability between AVCE and A level. This comparability and an attempt to broaden the curriculum was to be based on:

• emphasis within GNVQ on the academic requirements of vocational education

- the introduction of Advanced Subsidiary (AS) examinations as the first year of study prior to a second year leading to A2 examinations. The intent was that young people would study four or five subjects in their first year post-16 and then specialize in three or four subjects leading to A2.
- the modularization of all AS/A2 and AVCE examinations to form a mix-and-match structure.

The new structure and the new specifications were introduced in September 2000. Criticism of the proposals emphasized the remaining centrality of the academic focus, the bureaucracy of the assessment systems, and the potential impact on both students and teachers of the teaching and learning intensity required by creating a system that required three 'high-stakes' assessment periods in three years (GCSE at 16, AS at 17 and A2 at 18) (Torrance and Coultas, 2004). Balanced against this was the view that the new system did indeed enhance flexibility and the creation of individually tailored programmes for full-time students, and the opportunity to defer critical 'narrowing' programme and subject choices by one year. The first full cycle of Curriculum 2000 was examined in summer 2002, but was surrounded by controversies about marking standards and the impact of workload on young people (Tait et al., 2002). These concerns precipitated yet another review of the whole 14–19 curriculum, therefore, through the Tomlinson review, and the confusion engendered by the prospect of rapid change and reform returned. The battle of the 14–19 curriculum continues.

Reality check

At the political, systemic and organizational levels this review has stressed a number of key features of the curriculum debate since 1979:

1. The ritual of promoting vocational innovation while at the same time entrenching the reality and the market value of academic pathways.
2. The exclusion of young people from the process of reform and review.
3. Experimentation and change has led to intense turbulence and considerable confusion amongst key stakeholders.

But what about the reality, on the ground, for young people – what does the curriculum look like 'bottom up' from a young person's viewpoint?

The pathways facing a 14-year-old in 1979 were different in detail from those facing a 14-year-old in 2004, but in principle were much the same. The key difference is that remaining within a formal educational setting is now a much more likely 'choice' and that the pathways through that full-time education are greater in number and more diverse. Let us consider the 14–19 curriculum from the perspective of four young people from across the achievement range.

Our first 14-year-old is in the top 25 per cent of the achievement range and will pursue GCSEs, with brief work experience at age 15. Having obtained seven to ten GCSEs at Grade C or better he or she will progress to a programme of four or five AS levels followed by a year taking three subjects at A2. Within this programme some core skills, will have been included to ensure achievement across literacy, numeracy and information technology (IT) to NVQ Level 2. At 18 our 'top 25' student will enter university to study for a degree.

Our second 14-year-old is in the second quartile. He or she will take the same GCSE programme as the 'top 25' student, but will achieve five to seven Grades A–C. Post-16 education will take place in a school sixth form or a sixth form college and will comprise mostly A levels, but with some including an AVCE in place of two A levels. At 18, about half of this group will proceed to university, probably to one of the new universities rather than a traditional redbrick or civic university, so our young person stands a 50 per cent chance of progressing to become a graduate at 21. Alternatively he or she will leave formal education at 18 to enter employment.

The third 14-year-old is in the third quartile. He or she will still follow a GCSE pathway, but including some vocational GCSEs or even a foundation GNVQ in business or IT. At 16 our young person will achieve eight or nine graded GCSEs, with one to four of them at Grade C or better. The choices at 16 will then be substantial, for he or she will choose either to pursue vocational education in a school or post-16 college – normally through AVCE programmes or other vocational courses – or to enter training through a Modern Apprenticeship. It is here that the reality of the confusion and complexity of 16–19 is most visible, and where the choices are most challenging. In either case, much of the 16–19 period will be spent in an educational environment, and at 17 or 18 our student will formally enter the labour market. There is a small chance that pursuing a GNVQ pathway will provide a pathway to university entrance, probably to pursue a vocationally focused undergraduate degree at a new university or a college of higher education.

Our final 14-year-old is in the lowest quartile of the achievement range. He or she has been supported through Key Stage 3 in school with additional teaching support, but is unmotivated by the academic curriculum of Key Stage 4 or is unable to engage fully with it. His or her programme will combine GCSEs in core subjects such as Mathematics or English with some vocational courses. For many the work-related curriculum will become increasingly important, and part of each week may be spent on vocational courses at a local FE college. At 16 our student will obtain a few graded GCSEs, but none at Grade C or better, and will be faced with a choice of either more education in vocational courses, probably at a further education college, or a job with training that includes NVQ-focused courses. An alternative, though, is to disengage with education or training and to take a job without any form of training attached or, in the case of some 8 per cent of the cohort, to become NEET – not in employment, education or training (Godfrey et al., 2002).

Our analysis of curriculum 14–19 has inevitably painted a broad picture of patterns, trends and changes. The experiences of individual young people are unique, and we would not wish to imply in our cameos that such pathways are inevitable and unchangeable. Perhaps one of the real achievements of recent curriculum change is that doors are not closed so early or irrevocably for young people, and at any stage it is possible to rejoin a particular pathway or change from the one you are on. The concepts of lifelong learning and widening participation are premised on the social justice perspective that underachievement at an early stage should not condemn an individual to lifelong failure. Nevertheless, the patterns we describe are the reality. The primacy of academic curricula and the struggle to create effective systems and models for other curricula and to connect them to the high-status academic pathways are the main themes of our account, and the concern about the risks of social exclusion for young people in the lowest quartile is considerable. For most young people there is little coherence and clarity about progression through 14–19. The exception is for those pursuing academic pathways throughout, where coherence is clear since this is the model that originally underpinned '14–19', and still persists today. In the chapters that follow we explore some more detailed implications of this narrative.

Chapter 5

Mind the gap: the vocational and academic divide

Values, ideology and the academic/vocational divide

Running through the curriculum reforms of the last quarter century, described in detail in Chapter 4, has been the ever-present rhetoric of the desire to narrow or close the apparent divide between academic and vocational pathways in 14–19. We have chosen to focus on this issue separately, in part because it has a significant impact on the structure and characteristics of the output and outcomes from the education and training enterprise. However, we also believe that recognizing the reality of the divide and the way it will continue to shape the education and training market may help in seeking ways of narrowing it more effectively than previous policy has managed. The emergence and nature of the vocational/academic divide will be explored as a background to understanding the policies and strategies employed to integrate the traditionally separate pathways and to equalize the market and cultural value ascribed to each. We shall also consider what it all means for young people.

The divide between academic and vocational pathways in education and training is deep-rooted within education and social systems, and has a long history. Indeed, Coffey (1992) traces its origin back to ancient Greece where the division into general (liberal) education and vocational (utilitarian) education was well established. The tradition in England of formal education is one of liberal academic education, a notion in which is strongly rooted much of the educational policy of the twentieth century (see Chapter 2) – the earliest schools, typically public schools, had a curriculum rooted in the classics, and the purpose of education was explicitly not vocational. The traditions of the public schools evolved into the curricula of the grammar schools in the twentieth century, and the curriculum for almost all children in all schools persists through to today as essentially academically focused. Vocational education, rather, was traditionally done outside formal education through skill development on the job or through traditional apprenticeship models.

There are few academic or policy documents on education or training within the 14–19 phase which do not point to the academic/vocational divide as a 'problem'. At first sight the issue is a straightforward one of contrasting value and status, summarized by Young (1996, p. 101) when he writes that: 'The barriers confronting attempts to enhance the status and content of vocational alternatives are … severe … (We) must face the fact, regardless of their content, that vocational qualifications are judged by employers and university admissions tutors as inferior.' The problem, though, is not just an educational one. The vocational/academic debate is not simply a discussion about how the education and training system should be organized, and the value of different pathways. It is, rather, a fundamental discussion for society as a whole about the nature and purpose of education, the relationship between education, economy and society, and the allocation of power and status (economic and cultural) within society. The apparent battlefield on which these arguments are fought in relation to 14–19 education and training represents simply the site of a skirmish in a wider political and ideological war being waged not just within the UK but across the globe. King (1993, p. 210), for example, highlights the 'lowly status of vocational and technical (education) especially in OECD countries', and suggests that the debates about power, economy and society that relate to this arena are truly international in their spread.

Education and socio-political power are inseparable. Apple (2004, p. 180) expresses clearly the connection between what is taught, valued and prioritized in our education/training system and the exercise of social and economic power: 'What something is, what it does, one's evaluation of it – all this is not naturally preordained. It is socially constructed … (They) are the results of political, economic and cultural activities, battles and compromises. They are conceived, designed and authored by real people with real interests.' The schism between vocational and academic learning in education and training cannot be conceived, therefore, as a natural, organic 'fact', but is the product of the evolution of systems that prioritized certain forms of learning over others to establish or confirm social structures.

The divide between vocational and academic pathways post-14 is complex. While the explicit expression of the divide is that the pathways lead to different qualifications and require different curricula and assessment methods, it is in the implicit facets of the divide that fundamental issues lie. Each of the pathways, and each of the key elements of terminology, is imbued with the characteristics of a number of moral, ideological and philosophical values, and it is these values that are the lens through which the 'divide' is usually regarded. Perhaps more importantly, these values themselves are characterized by polarized perspectives that risk simple separation of alternatives into 'black and white' or 'good and bad'. Hence no perspective on this 'divide' can be easily separated from implicit, and frequently explicit, judgements about the nature, character and social status of individuals, whether they be the young people involved, the teachers or trainers on their programmes, the policy-makers and managers within organizations or the employers/educational organizations to which the young people subsequently progress. The academic/vocational divide is essentially a divide of cultural capital. Vocational pathways and achievements are more frequently associated with those deemed not able to pursue an academic pathway, and destined to work in careers and at employment levels with lower social cachet. Academic pathways are the *habitus* of middle-class and aspirant middle-class social groups, while vocational pathways are popularly perceived as the *habitus* of working-class social groups. Academic pathways are perceived as the route to high-income employment; vocational pathways are often regarded as the route to lower income employment. The existence of definitive evidence for these polarities is not important in that they reflect perceptions ingrained in society norms and values. The very nature of what is vocational education has indeed changed over time.

To understand many of the dimensions of the academic/vocational divide it is necessary to consider the nature of vocationalism. We shall start by being critical of the simplicity of the debate, in that much of the issue lies in the limited understanding of the ideas and the terminologies involved. Indeed, Young (1996, p. 118) contends that a major difficulty in educational policy evolution in England and Wales in this field may be the semantic problems of the language that is used. Specifically, in English there is no simple word to integrate all aspects of learning and development equivalent to the French word *formation* and the German word *bildung*, and 'most of the terms and concepts which we have for discussing education and training ... have limiting and often highly divisive meanings'.

Part of the problem lies in the popular understanding of key terms, in that 'academic' and 'vocational' are narrowly defined as relating either to 'learning with the mind' and 'learning with the hands', respectively, or to 'learning for the mind' or 'learning for the hands'. Such a polarity of perspective encourages debates about which pole is 'right' and which is 'wrong', and such simplistic arguments continue into current discussions of the virtues of different organizational approaches to education and learning. We might, rather, view vocational and academic as representing a wide spectrum of learning situations in which the combination of practical and intellectual skills with the acquisition of key knowledge and understanding come together. All learning contains elements of both – the student of philosophy uses a wide range of intellectual and thinking skills in his or her enterprise, while the trainee hairdresser requires significant knowledge of procedures, regulations and essential scientific concepts. Pring (1995) has emphasized what he describes as the absurdity of the polarity of view of academic and vocational for, as Marples (1996, p. 67), indicates: '(There is) an untenable distinction between theory and practice, as if each is impervious to the other, and that people engaged in practical activities require little or nothing from what theory has to offer, or vice versa.'

Coffey (1992), for example, has shown how the vocational education of one era can become the academic education of another, and cites the example of classics, developed initially as vocational education for intending clerics and lawyers but subsequently forming the essence of academic education. We might see similar changes in the status of science education during the twentieth century. We must also note one of the interesting tensions in the debate about vocational and academic pathways or curricula. The notion that vocational pathways focus on utility in relation to employment and the economy is a key plank in government policy both in England and across the globe. However, as many writers have pointed out (for example Gleeson, 1990) there is a strong paradox in this argument in that: 'The courses giving the broadest range of vocational access are the academic courses. Vocational courses narrow choice and, at the lower levels, may never lead to actual employment' (Cockett and Callaghan, 1996, p. 34).

Similarly, any distinction between the vocational and the academic on the grounds of ultimate utility is misleading, where vocational activity is seen as a preparation for economic (working) life. The boundaries between economic life and all other aspects of an individual's life are blurred at best, and may be perceived as becoming even more so in the twenty-first century. Distinguishing how far specific skills or knowledge feeds only one element of an individual's existence is inevitably problematic.

Issues across the divide

We have focused so far on some of the philosophical dimensions of the academic/vocational divide. But why is the existence of such a divide a problem? The purposes of any education and training system will be, at least in part, to meet the economic and social needs of contemporary and future society, so if the system meets those needs then there would be little rationale for change, however interesting the philosophical debate. The argument is clearly signalled that the divide creates a set of problems for those organizing our education and training system and those young people who pass through the system. It is important to stress, of course, that any social system is in large measure the product of evolutionary change from some earlier state or format, and the inherent conservative nature of most systems, the inertia of existing structures and systems, and the time required to initiate and implement change mean that there is always a discrepancy between current systems and current needs. Decisions to change the system to meet today's needs will inevitably not be in place until some future date, by which time the needs themselves will have moved on. Education and training systems are inevitably time-lagged systems in their responsiveness. We might expect to see that the current system does not fully meet current needs, but is changing in the direction of meeting them in the future. We need, therefore, to consider what the concerns are about the vocational/academic divide.

The issues associated with the vocational/academic divide relate particularly to the fact that such a division not only does not meet the current needs of society and the economy, but is in fact inimical to them in many ways. Writing in the early 1990s, the Institute for Public Policy Research (1990) identified five key weaknesses with a divided system, such as that which characterizes England and Wales.

First, the divide represents the view that manual labour and intellectual work are discrete and separate roles within the economy, a form of economic organization often termed 'divisive specialization'. The origins of this perspective lie in the industrialization of the nineteenth and early twentieth centuries and the emergence of mass-production methods, Fordism, and Taylorian management methods. Within such systems there existed a marked division of labour between planning, organization and management on the one hand, and the physical process of production on the other (Piore and Sabel, 1984). This division of labour translated directly into the organization of training and education, with the development of the intellectual skills for management undertaken through the academic school system, and the development of skills for manual labour developed through work-based training, normally by employers, for those selected not to continue in formal education beyond the minimum school-leaving age. Essentially, we may suggest that the mass education system emerged in the same era as industrialization, and so is structured to meet the economic needs of what is now an anachronistic model of social and economic organization.

The concern is that the economic and social needs of the twenty-first century are focused on the development, understanding and application of knowledge, rather than such divisions of labour, and should be organized so that responsiveness is rapid and flexible. This may be seen as the product of globalization and the dominance of a global economic system but, whatever its origin, it is regarded by government as the key driving force in shaping how social and economic systems might be organized. Castells (1989, quoted in Young, 1996, p. 116) has indicated that: 'social institutions … will be key elements in fostering or stalling the new productive forces. The more a society facilitates the exchange of information flows, the decentralised generation and distribution of information, the greater will be its collective symbolic capacity'. The need for productive social systems, such as the education and training system, to both model and provide preparation for such organization in the economy and society is a key perspective in the push to narrow or demolish the academic/vocational divide. As Young (1996, p. 116) suggests, 'a high participation education system linked to a high skill system of production would require a curriculum which was congruent with it'.

Secondly, the divide is founded on the notion of selection, where the ability or inclination to proceed with academic study was the key criterion for selection into those heading for higher-status managerial and professional roles in society. In the economic and social structures of the nineteenth and early twentieth centuries the numbers needed in the 'intellectual' and leadership roles in society were relatively small, and a twin-track education system, with key selection points at 11, at school-leaving age and at university entrance provided the narrow gateways to the academic pathways. Finegold and Soskice (1988) have stressed that the existence of a twin-track system based on the award of qualifications of different status will inevitably mean that the system is predominantly focused on its selection function – identifying which young people are suited to higher education and which should directly enter employment.

The need to engage much larger proportions of the population into knowledge-based employment, requiring higher levels of education and training, means that a system based on selection may be inappropriate for the economic needs of the state.

Thirdly, separation into two pathways at an early stage of young people's education produces an inherently inflexible system. Those in each may be limited, by structural constraints and 'labelling', to the opportunities within that pathway. This has implications both for the individual and for society as a whole. For the individual it militates against late development, changing perspectives or those constrained in some way by personal circumstances as they pass through the school system. For society it raises issues of equity, but also constrains the responsiveness of society and the economy to changing external environments. The ability of individuals, organizations and society to respond positively and rapidly to new opportunities or positive or negative economic or social change is considerably constrained.

Fourthly, it fails to recognize the connectedness of intellectual and operational practical skills in the processes of innovation. In all economic systems societal advance is, at least in part, premised on technological change, yet technological change requires the intellectual skills of creativity, problem-solving and the management of change and innovation, and the practical operational skills of engineering and production. While specialism is still desirable and inevitable in both broad fields, the presence in all individuals of some degree of both sets of skills is inevitably more efficient and beneficial. As Young (1996, p. 110) suggests, the academic/vocational divide 'inhibits innovative combinations that can link theoretical and applied studies'.

Fifthly, it reinforces the social stratification of society, for the routes are clearly distinguished as high-status academic routes and low-status vocational routes. This is not just an issue of equity, and hence a moral issue, but is also an issue in relation to its impact on those social problems that arise from a highly polarized society. Reay (2001b, p. 344), *inter alia*, has suggested that this is a particular issue for society in Britain, where:

> Far from developing a classless society, the English educational system is still prey, in the twenty-first century, to Tawney's 'curse' (1938) of being organised along lines of social class. Historically, the working classes have constantly been 'found out' in education; discovered to be inferior, less cultured, less clever than the middle

classes … Both finding and losing yourself are about a lack in relation to the academic.

The generation of social groups likely to be excluded from the mainstream of society is a key political concern, and was the driver for the establishment of the government's Social Exclusion Unit.

These five concerns have emerged persistently in both academic and government policy debate throughout the 1990s. Each is a deep-rooted issue resistant to simple solutions, since the changes required to overcome them are not confined to organization and operation within the education system itself. Rather, they require fundamental social change, and changes in the perceptions and attitudes of employers, parents, politicians and young people themselves. We shall examine below the steps that have been taken to address some of these issues, before we consider how young people themselves see it all.

Bridging the divide

Overall, two basic strategies have been used to try to address the issues arising from the division of vocational and academic pathways, and these have been identified by the Institute for Public Policy Research (1990), as the 'German solution' and the 'French solution', reflecting their emergence in other European countries. The German solution is to try to raise the status and profile of vocational qualifications to ensure that they are regarded as the equal of academic awards. The focus here is on working within the vocational system rather than dealing with issues in the academic pathway. The French solution is to 'diversify the academic track to give it broader appeal and make it less exclusive' (Young, 1996, p. 109), or to work principally to modify the model and structure of academic pathways to ensure they integrate vocational themes and strands within them. Both models have been used within the education and training system in England, to some degree in parallel, but with two distinct phases of activity.

The first approach was essentially to use the German solution. It is with the development of vocational education and training beyond basic craft levels and within formal educational settings that the academic/vocational divide has become an issue of focus and concern. In the beginning the only educational routeways were academic ones, and the emergence of NVQs and GNVQs in the late 1980s and throughout the 1990s has been an attempt to raise the profile of vocational awards. Academic tracks were available only to a relatively small, select number. Selection at age 11, at age 16 and at age 18 into smaller and smaller groups of academic elite endowed on to academic pathways a high social and economic value. Vocational education was for those who left school at the earliest opportunity or who were not selected for academic pathways, and in itself was often very brief 'learning on the job'. Comparatively few young people ever undertook a formal craft apprenticeship.

We might characterize the last quarter of the twentieth century as the rise of vocationalism. Its growth was a deliberate attempt both to provide alternate education and training pathways and to meet labour market needs at higher and higher levels, and as such emerged as an alternative to academic education. But any new entrant into a market must compete strongly with the existing market leaders, and vocationalism had a major challenge to meet the market primacy of academic education. At first it sought not to compete, but simply to provide an alternative for those not pursuing academic pathways. As the levels of achievement that could be reached through formal vocational education and training increased, though, it was clear that at most levels through 14–19 education there were both vocational and academic options. Vocationalism sought, at this stage, to establish itself in the market on the basis of being different, and of emphasizing practice-based work and competency-based assessment. With the introduction of GNVQs in the early 1990s, vocationalism made its ultimate pitch to be an equal but different pathway through to the holy grail of education, the university place.

Even with political promotion by government of this notion, though, the market dominance of academic education remained, nurtured principally by the recognition that the route into the most highly regarded universities remained the academic route. While vocational routes could lead to vocationally focused degree programmes at 'new' universities and colleges, the high-status single honours degrees in classical academic disciplines at established universities remained the territory of the academically educated middle classes. The 'me-different' approach to the market failed fundamentally to shift the perception of the long-term relative value of vocational and academic routeways. Raffe (1985) and Cockett (1996) have both suggested that such an approach to curriculum innovation, of building new programmes from the bottom of the achievement scale for those young people not currently well served, are likely to fail, for two reasons.

First, any course takes on the social status of the young people recruited to it, so any new course designed for the lowest achievers will simply continue their position not change it. Secondly, 'courses which are based on a vocational promise that they will prepare pupils for the world of work face a further problem ... in that employers will recruit what they see to be the best available students and their measure for this continues to be examination success' (Cockett, 1996, p. 45).

Once a system has been established that can provide awards at all the levels that academic awards can be achieved, however, the second phase has been to seek ways of ensuring integration and connectedness between the two systems. The establishment of the QCA, the emergence of Curriculum 2000 and the proposals that have emerged from the Tomlinson review all demonstrate a strong shift towards the French solution. This recognizes the need to adopt a strategy of disguise to raise the profile of vocational elements of the curriculum and vocational pathways, to construct them in a way that their detail may be hidden from some of the end-users. To this end the growth of GNVQs and the subsequent establishment of Curriculum 2000 was a deliberate attempt by the government to cause the relationship between the two perspectives to shift. In effect the government recognized that enhancing the status of vocational education and training would only arise from emphasizing the mutual benefits of the connections with academic paths. Vocational programmes were still seen to be different, but their similarities and overlaps with academic education became a key focus, with combination between them seen as virtuous and important. Integrating vocational dimensions (for example, key skills) into academic programmes, or enabling young people to study vocational areas through academic approaches (as in many aspects of GNVQs) began to break down public perceptions of a schism between the two arenas.

The learner's view

The implications of this for choice by young people are significant. Where do they stand in this complex ideological battleground, and how can they make the choices that they are now required to make? Choosing one pathway rather than the other aligns the individual with the values and expectations associated with that route. To choose a vocational pathway is to choose a set of labels that will secure acceptability within certain social groupings and explicit rejection by those in or aspiring to be in others. Choosing between academic and vocational pathways must be seen, therefore, as choosing to be defined as part of a particular social group, which will work its way out in terms of pathways, expectations and likely achievements throughout the rest of the individual's life. In many ways, therefore, it is a life and lifestyle decision, not simply an educational one. Choosing to move out of the social setting and social values in which an individual has been brought up and steeped is likely to be a difficult decision for adults with substantial life experience. For young people in their mid-teenage years it may be a challenge that is far too difficult to consider, resulting in the replication of existing social patterns associated with vocational and academic pathways. Furthermore, if 'academic' pathways have the high social status, there is little moral dilemma for those young people (and their parents) from the social groupings where such pathways are the norm. The real challenge is for those whose family and social traditions lie in vocational areas and pathways, but who may recognize that it is only by choosing to move into academic educational pathways that access to higher socio-economic status can be achieved. Not only do they have a decision of 'change' to make, but they may also possess fewer of the elements of cultural capital to facilitate that change. This can provide a major barrier to mobility between the two arenas. Even if they choose to pursue a vocational pathway, the range and diversity of choice is complex and daunting, and in consequence 'some are lost in an apparent jungle of alternative courses and qualifications, too many of which lack status, clarity of purpose and brand recognition with employers' (DfES, 2003h, p. 11).

If a key aim of government policy since 1979 has been the narrowing of the academic/vocational divide, then there is little real evidence that this has been achieved in any substantial way from the students' view. Indeed, we have argued in an earlier chapter that the effect of most of the strategies has been to replicate rather than replace the 'old order' and to provide more ways in which young people, parents, employers and higher education can pursue academic pathways to success. It might be argued that such entrenched social values will take substantial periods of time to break down. By the end of the 1980s, and after a concerted period of activity to raise the profile and value of vocational pathways Davies was disappointed to note from his research with 16–18-year-olds that: 'In contrast with A-levels, (vocational courses) had a much less attractive image to those who chose the (academic) route. ... Once again these findings are symptomatic of the relative difference in public esteem in which the types of qualifications are currently held' (Davies, 1993, p. 14).

The impact of policy and practice in the 1990s was similarly unsuccessful in changing attitudes. Foskett and Hesketh's national study of the decision-making of 16-year-olds in relation to further education demonstrated the primacy of gaining entry to higher education as an influencer in that process, and that consciousness of the academic/vocational dichotomy was an important factor in choice. They report (Foskett and Hesketh, 1997, p. 316) that:

> In our data we have seen clear evidence of the prejudicial attitudes of young people towards vocational qualifications ... Such feelings appear to stem from the distrust shown by young people in the capacity of vocational qualifications to deliver what most sixth form students today aspire to: higher education. It is not so much the perception that A-levels are more likely to facilitate university entrance, but the more serious assumption that vocational qualifications are not a recognised path to university. Despite Dearing's recommendation that universities should make clear their support of vocational qualifications when reaching decisions on recruitment, young people have made clear their own thoughts on the academic/vocational divide by voting with their feet.

Reality check

The last two decades have seen a strong focus on the vocational/academic divide. Coffey (1992) has suggested that a high profile for this particular debate is always linked closely to periods of economic challenge, and that the debate wanes during periods of economic stability. It is clear that there has been a concerted effort by governments of all political persuasions to narrow the divide or bridge the gap between the two sides of the chasm, and that a range of strategies have been used to make progress. However, the entrenched views of key stakeholders are still easy to see. Despite the logical requirement that an effective and economically successful labour force comprises individuals with skills and knowledge from across the academic/vocational spectrum, the reality is that the academic/vocational divide is a social and cultural structure that serves a wide range of social purposes beyond education and training. As such it may change only on scales of generations and not within the time horizons of governments. This is not a resigned perspective that suggests nothing can change. Indeed, we would stress that there is an imperative on government, education professionals and other stake-holders to take action that places all young people at the centre of the 14–19 system, and not just those privileged by social class and back-ground. This requires recognition of the fact that little fundamental change has been achieved by the policies of the last 25 years in relation to curriculum, and that the rhetoric of change must be matched by more radical actions. Indeed, as Bourdieu (1993, p. 629) indicates (quoted in Reay, 2001b):

> If it is true that it is not easy to eliminate or even modify most of the economic and social factors behind the worst suffering … it is also true that any political programme that fails to take advantage of the possibilities for action … can be considered guilty of nonassistance to a person in danger.

We might suggest that the ritual dance between vocational and academic partners continues to be bashful and tentative, with neither partner enthusiastic in embracing the other fully. Each is suspicious of the other's true intents, and each is concerned about the impact on their future profile and the credibility of being seen to mix with the other. There remains a lot of progress to be made before they embrace fully and we can approach a position of parity of esteem between vocational and academic pathways.

Chapter 6

Teaching and learning: the learner's perspective

What is it all for?

One of the widely held conceptions discussed in Chapter 2 was that participation in education and training has grown. In fact, what has changed is the location of learning away from the workplace into educational institutions, from 48 per cent in 1989 to 71 per cent in 2002. This relocation has led to an imperative to accommodate the needs of a much wider range of young people within schools and colleges. The wider range of learners staying in full-time education or training has exerted a pressure to adapt teaching which is dominated by an academic curriculum, a pressure felt throughout Key Stage 4. Young people themselves have also changed, with large numbers in part-time work (42 per cent of 14-year-olds, 80 per cent of 18–19-year-olds [Hodgson and Spours, 2001]), and a consequent view of education as one significant element in their lives, but by no means necessarily the primary element.

Has this then led to a change in the conceptualization of the purpose and the practice of teaching and learning? In other words, have we reconsidered what it is all for and how to do it?

The rhetoric of purpose

The OECD presents statements of the purpose of education and training as focusing primarily on the development of the individual, the liberal humanist approach as defined in Chapter 4:

> How to ensure that employment concerns are reconciled in a balanced way with the full development of individuals as citizens, voters, family and community members, and human beings? (OECD, 1992, p. 71)

... consensus begins to be forged that education and training, including in the early formative years, must promote such attributes as curiosity, independence and leadership, ability to co-operate, tolerance, industriousness, and problem solving under conditions of uncertainty ... (OECD, 1992, p. 104)

However, analysts of education discern quite different aims, reflecting instrumental and classical humanist approaches, primarily concerned with serving the purpose not of the individual, but of society and the economy:

- To transmit the kinds of knowledge and skills required to sustain industrial economies, especially the scientific and technical knowledge on which they were based.
- To reinforce prevailing cultural values in society – the beliefs and attitudes to which people were expected to conform.
- To select the people most fitted to fill the roles which society needed, and allocate them to an appropriate status or position in society
- To reconcile people's aspirations with social needs so that they accepted their place in society (Jarvis et al., 2003, pp. 17–18).

Such conclusions are founded on the work of sociologists such as Bernstein (1977) who stress the function of education as one of control and maintenance of the dominant group. In counterpoise to stated aspirations about equality of opportunity in education are analyses which argue that the continuation of inequality, for example, in terms of race (McLean, 1995) or gender (Bryson, 1999), is necessary for the continuation of a capitalist and/or patriarchal society, and are embedded in the practice of education. This chapter considers two contrary perspectives, that education for 14–19-year-olds is about ensuring success for all, based on the primary aim of developing the individual's potential, or that it is about the selection of an elite, with the primary aim of serving the dominant group through servicing the economy in its current constitution. This chapter will consider these two views through the perspective of teaching and learning and how teaching and learning are experienced by young people themselves.

Take 100 young people

Conceptions of the experience of teaching and learning of young people are shaped by the dominant perception of the 'typical' schoolchild, seen as studying the National Curriculum and progressing to GCSEs and from there, remaining in school to do A levels followed by entry into university, the top 25 per cent of the achievement range highlighted in Chapter 4. However, this pathway is not relevant to very many young people who absent themselves physically or psychologically, or are excluded. The 2 per cent of young people with statements of special educational needs (SEN) and the 13 per cent in secondary schools without a statement but with SEN (DfES, 2003f) may also not be following the assumed common pathway. The majority is also often assumed to remain in school until 18. In fact, figures from the DfES (2003g) show this to be a misconception. In 2002, of a hundred 16-year-olds, only 18 are typically likely to stay in a state-funded school and four in a public school. The remainder will go elsewhere. The largest group, 23, will in fact go to a further education or sixth form college. Eight are likely to go to some form of work-based learning and four to employer-funded training. A fair sized group, eight, will become NEET – not in education, employment or training (Godfrey et al., 2002). Unfortunately the assumed 'typical' pathway outlined above has led to the creation of a norm, and young people who do not follow this path or for whom it is not relevant may be seen as somehow 'remedial' (Raffo, 2003), and in need of gathering into the mainstream fold.

The fault lines described above between the norm and the perceived deviant are reflected in the experience of teaching and learning. The pattern of adaptation of teaching and learning has tended towards the maintenance of a hegemonic pathway with peripheral initiatives to either allow those for whom the pathway is not suited to participate to some degree, or initiatives to encourage those who have voluntarily opted out, to opt back in. An example of the former is the establishment of a National Curriculum which did not take account of those with moderate learning difficulties (MLD), just under half of those with a statement of special educational needs. Costley (1996) discovered that less than a third of teachers of learners with MLD felt the aims of the National Curriculum matched those of their school. They were faced with the difficult choice of disapplying elements of the curriculum, so taking young people out of what was perceived as the national entitlement, or struggling to adapt content and assessment to fit their pupils' needs. An example of the second strategy of 'come back in' is the various projects to offer education outside of a school environment, often individually or vocationally based, with the intended outcome of re-entry into or re-engagement with mainstream schooling. How has the maintenance of an assumed majority pathway, plus additional strategies for those outside the fold, the norm plus approach, been reflected in the actual practice of pedagogy, that is 'any conscious activity by one person designed to enhance learning in another' (Watkins and Mortimore, 1999, p. 3)?

Teaching and learning

Views on teaching and learning for 14–19-year-olds are generated externally, by inspections for example, and internally from young people themselves. The 2001 *Annual Report* of the Office for Standards in Education (OFSTED) concludes that:

> In Key Stage 4 the teaching is good or better in nearly four fifths of schools ... Across the key stages the teaching is now unsatisfactory in fewer than one school in twenty-five ...
>
> The principal strength of teaching remains teachers' knowledge and understanding of the subjects they teach. Skills in managing pupils are generally strong, being satisfactory or better in about 19 out of 20 schools. (OFSTED, 2003, paras 75–76)

The accompanying commentary makes clear an implicit model of good teaching, with clear learning objectives explained at the commencement of a lesson, a tightly structured process of teaching and a plenary at the end restating what has been learned. There is little room for lessons which start from the students' interests or needs as articulated by them, rather than interpreted and decided by the teacher, who in turn is restricted by the National Curriculum framework.

The OFSTED generally optimistic view of teaching and learning is reflected to some extent in the views of young people. Despite some mistrust of their views and the belief that they are not competent to make judgements (Ashworth, 1995), their opinions are generally positive (Blatchford, 1996; Thomas et al., 2000). However, within the largely affirmative feedback, there are corners of disturbing disagreement. For example, within the study carried out by Thomas et al. (2000), comprising the views of 3,552 secondary school pupils, 48 per cent found school always or sometimes boring, 21 per cent felt teachers never or hardly ever listened and 35 per cent felt teachers never or hardly ever told them how they were getting on. Similarly in Blatchfords's study, 25 per cent of 16-year-olds felt the worst thing about school was problems with particular lessons. Why then, if as OFSTED suggest, poor teaching and learning is relatively rare, are a sizeable minority of learners not in agreement?

Learning

Analysis and discussion of learning necessarily atomizes the process in order to allow understanding of a highly complex process. The literature is scattered with polarities, pedagogy/androgogy, formal/informal learning, situated/context specific, or spectra charting the place of a particular approach to teaching or learning on a continuum. There are suggestions that one form of learning is superior to another in offering an emancipatory experience, or greater transferability, or status. The discussion may be founded on political and/or pedagogic analysis. The appropriateness of approaches to teaching for those of different socio-economic classes, learning styles and age is dissected, as are their impact on life trajectories. However, increasingly, simple dichotomies or single points on a scale are challenged as misrepresenting the complexity of the teaching and learning process, and this section of the chapter will examine some of the tensions in the current debate.

Questions about the control and transferability of learning invoke complex answers, nowhere more so than for 14–19 education and training. Teaching and learning of 14–19-year-olds is shaped by the dominance of school teaching. Assumptions are made about the nature of teaching relevant to those who are considered still children and the sort of teaching likely to achieve success in the context of the framework of the National Curriculum and a strongly credentialist system. Questions of control, related to the need to take charge of and protect children, inevitably raise questions concerning whether the control is used for other ends also, particularly to use power over young people to advantage or disadvantage individuals and groups. Within the debate on the nature and process of learning, androgogy and pedagogy are sometimes presented as alternatives relevant to learners of different ages, as in Table 6.1.

The underlying assumptions of androgogy charted in Table 6.1 are that adults are self-motivated, self-directing and bring to learning a rich range of experience on which to build. Pedagogy, by contrast, assumes children are in need of direction and control, and bring little in the way of experience to the process. Such an easy division is largely discredited. For decades it has been recognized that the two approaches to teaching and

Table 6.1 *The assumptions of andragogy*

	Pedagogical	Andragogical
Concept of the learner	Dependent personality	Increasingly self-directed
Role of learner's experience	To be built on, more than used as a resource	A rich resource for learning by self and other
Reading to learn	Uniform by age, level and curriculum	Develops from life tasks and problems
Orientation to learning	Subject centred	Task or problem-centred
Motivation	By external rewards and punishment	By internal incentives and curiosity

Source: Knowles, 1984, p. 116
(Quoted in Armitage, et al., 1984: 64)

Table 6.2 *Minton's matrix of control*

Teacher control		
		Lecture
		Demonstration
		Discussion (structured)
	Less control	Discussion (unstructured)
		Seminar
		Tutorial
	Shared control	Practical
		Simulation and games
		Role-play
		Resource-based learning
		Films/television programmes
		Visits
	Student control	Distance learning/flexi-study
		Discovery projects/ research
Least control		Real-life experience

Source: Minton, 1991: 112, cited in Armitage et al., 1999: 77

learning do not relate to the age of the learner but, rather, to the nature of the learning objective, and both styles may be relevant at any age (Davenport, 1993; Elias, 1979). However, the apparently politically neutral dichotomy, in its assumption of the necessity for control in the case of younger learners, inevitably invites consideration of the political implications. If the locus of control is a central issue, then what are the values and intentions of those in control? Similarly, categorizations of learning into more or less directed forms also have political resonance in suggesting how far the individual can be allowed to shape and direct their own learning or how far they are subject to the power of others. Minton suggests a spectrum of control reflected in teaching techniques as indicated in Table 6.2.

In this way, teaching techniques, such as role-play, take on the mantle of a political perspective in apparently opening or limiting the control of learning by the learner or teacher. A further dimension of analysis is where learning takes place. Colley et al. (2003) chart the assumptions that learning in the workplace or the community is different to that in 'formal' education organizations along a number of dimensions (Table 6.3). This analysis locates a very high degree of structure, and certification as a primary aim within schools and colleges. Workplace training is characterized as less structured. Its ongoing informal learning happens outside formal structures. Colley et al. (2003, para. 5, Executive Summary) while noting that 'all forms of learning have the potential to be either emancipatory or oppressive', argue against demonizing formal didactic teaching and oversimplifying the differences between formal and informal learning. Nevertheless, there appears to be a default position within formal education which veers towards those styles of teaching and learning associated with pedagogy and formal teaching from which those facilitating learning for 14–19-year-olds struggle to diverge.

Increasingly, learning is understood as 'situated', that is, intimately

Table 6.3 *European Commission communication on lifelong learning: formal, non-formal and informal learning*

	Formal learning	Non-formal learning	Informal learning
Location	Education and training institutions	Not provided by an education and training institution. Bulk of learning occurs in the workplace Pre-school playgroups, etc. Community groups and voluntary sector	Daily activities at work, home, leisure, in community Youth organizations Intergenerational learning
Degree of Structure	Highly structured objectives, time and support	Structured objectives, time or support	No structure
Intentionality	Learner's perspective is intentional	Learner's perspective is intentional	Rarely intentional, typically 'incidental'
Certification	Leads to certification	Not usually certificated	Not certificated
Facilitator	Teacher/trainer	Trainer, coach, mentor, child-carer	

Source: Colley et al., 2003: 25

related to location and to the community within which the learning takes place. It follows there are debates about how far learning acquired in one setting, for example, school, can be transferred to another, such as work (Engestrom, 1991; Lave and Wenger, 1990). Research is probing how far the degree to which the values and culture of the community within which learning takes place are shared or attractive to the learner may influence the learning process. For example, Raffo (2003) suggests that for disaffected young people in Key Stage 4 to be re-engaged, there must be sufficient similarity between the values of the learner and those of the learning community. In such an environment the young person is able to establish the social and cultural ties with those around him or her which are essential to successful learning. Paechter (2001) suggests that schools are culturally alienating to many, and so structurally inhibit the possibilities for learning. She argues that there is a generally held belief that school knowledge is somehow 'different' to knowledge held in the wider world, and that it has high status and reflects the domain of an elite:

> School knowledge represents a narrow selection from wider possibilities, that selection being more influenced by the preservation of an elite group than by its usefulness to life in general. It is thus a subsection of the totality of the knowledge available and chosen mainly in order to preserve a particular social system, though this is of course rarely made explicit. (Paechter, 2001, p. 169)

Consequently, young people may be made to feel that they have little when in fact they may have considerable knowledge, just not the knowledge valued within schools. There is a dislocation between the world of the young person's family and work, and the world of the school, the latter appearing unreal to many. Colley et al. (2003) argue against polarizing the debate and the suggestion that certain forms of knowledge or locations for learning are innately superior. However, the weight of argument from research suggests that schools are stressful places for many 14–19-year-olds and are not experienced as a positive environment for learning (East Midlands Learning and Skills Research Network, 2002).

Teaching in action

Chapter 4 outlined changes in the curriculum since 1979, some of which it was argued were designed to facilitate a broader range of teaching methods, including competence acquisition and assessment, self-directed and resource-based learning. It was also suggested at the start of this chapter that a wider range of young people were staying in education beyond 16 and thereby influencing the curriculum and teaching not just at 16 and over, but earlier in Key Stage 4. It follows that changes in teaching should be discernible.

A study of young people's experience suggests that teaching and learning undergoes a sea change in year 10 (Harris et al., 1995). Up to this point, in years 7–9, work has been relatively relaxed, with a creative and experiential emphasis resulting in guided short pieces of work to be handed in immediately. As the GCSE syllabus begins in year 10, the quantity and pace of work increases, and demands are made for learners to manage their commitments and time, and to exercise new skills of note-taking, revision and examination. Enjoyment of learning decreases (ibid.). Young people experience this change as mysterious, in Harris et al.'s (1995, p. 256) phrase, they begin year 10 'paddling upstream in the dark'. They come to understand effective learning as learning the rules of the system and manipulating them, getting by and, above all, many equate working fast with working hard and working effectively. The aim is not to reflect or to understand, but to develop strategies that will allow them to cope with the volume and pace and to reproduce in examinations the knowledge transmitted by teachers.

In this study, some did not cope and were alienated by one or more features of the regime. They could not keep up with the pace. They were frustrated by being told they were not listening carefully enough, when they listened but did not understand. The exhortation to 'work harder' if they experienced problems did not help them, as it equated in their minds with working faster and, consequently, even less effectively. In another study, the pressure of frequent changes in focus, ruled by the bell signalling a period change is also experienced as oppressive. The change to a system in a college which is more relaxed and has fewer subjects is seen as liberating by one 15-year-old in a recent study (Lumby and Morrison, 2004, p. 10) for whom the pressure of learning in school was too much:

> Most people have difficulties at school. More people don't like school than like school. College is more enjoyable than school. Mainly it's the freedom you get. It's a lot, lot better. You don't feel like everybody is constantly in your face and you have got no freedom and there are too many boundaries … There is less pressure.

Those who feel excluded or alienated by this experience of 'learning' seek inclusion through their peer group. Also, Cuban (1993, p. 8) suggests the reason so many young people work is not only for financial reward but also, 'to search out meaningful attachment' which is not available to them at school.

Structure

Structurally, schools and colleges are driven by the overarching framework of the timetable and age stages. Learning is divided into blocks of time for learners grouped by age and generally into discrete subjects. The appropriateness of this framework to support learning is questioned. Bowring-Carr and West-Burnham characterize the secondary curriculum as:

- activity constrained by artificial periods of time which have no known correlation with any learning process (the 40-minute lesson)
- random sequencing of subjects
- block grouping of pupils based on one-dimensional criteria (that is, intelligence or ability)
- an emphasis on teaching to 'get through' syllabuses and schemes of work
- the design of activities to fit the time available rather than the needs of the children or the topic (Bowring-Carr and West-Burnham, 1997, pp. 69–70).

The rigidity and archaic nature of the structure has been deplored by many commentators (Boyd, 1997; Cuban, 1995; Pring, 1990; Stoll and Fink, 1996). It both a reflects the credentialist agenda and embeds it further. The structure has a number of results. Teachers feel driven by the demands of each subject and by a perception of lack of time to 'cover' the curriculum. The result is a focus on teaching not learning, and a retreat into teacher-centred rather than student-centred activities. The size of classes is also perceived as a pressure in this direction. The result is that of the four forms of teaching and learning outlined by Harris et al. (1995) – didactic transmission, experiential learning, creative learning, task-based learning – it is the first which dominates. Teachers feel they have no time to teach the skills needed for learning during this phase such as note-taking, but are sucked into methods focused, above all, on achieving credentials. As a result they engage in what Cuban (1993, pp. 4–5) terms 'pedagogical triage'. We have depicted 14–19 education as a battlefield. Just as in a war zone, those most likely to survive are treated while those who have a small or no chance are disregarded; pedagogical triage is a parallel process of prioritizing selection for attention. Teaching focuses on those who are the high flyers, those who may go up a grade, particularly D to C, and those who disrupt. Those of middle-level ability are the most likely to be left to their own devices.

Teachers perceive themselves as victims of externally imposed demands. Nevertheless, the perspective from the learners may be different. While they acknowledge that different subjects may offer different levels of leverage for varying teaching, the choice appears sometimes to reflect the personal predilection of the teacher, rather than an unavoidable effect of the curriculum and assessment regime. In a study of 16–18-year-olds, Lumby and Briggs (2002) found that the learner's experience was not consistent, and that learners' perceptions of the proportion of teachers willing to listen and respond to learners' views on learning varied across and within institutions. The study also showed that Mayne's (1992) finding that the teaching of A levels was largely whole-class and didactic was still evident in 2002, though it had become the experience of the minority. Many staff, responding to changes in the learner profile, to curriculum changes, for example the advent of GNVQ, and developing their own professional practice, had made strenuous efforts to vary teaching away from the whole-class didactic approach. In sixth form colleges:

> A wide range of tactics have been adopted to try to move from teaching a whole class to engineering time to help individuals learn:
>
> - ensuring that activities are varied and highly structured
> - concentrating on practical activities
> - providing additional individual support for those with learning difficulties
> - releasing students for blocks of time to do their own supported investigative work
> - workshops for additional support
> - use of LCD projection programmes on an intranet
> - use of simulation games and role play
> - more trips and residentials
> - open learning study guides
> - resource packs (updated by a dedicated team)
> - trading intranet materials with other colleges
> - the creative use of the new technology, including ICT and interactive whiteboards, to promote more independent learning and thereby free teacher time to assist individual students

- changing the examination board where necessary to ensure that external assessment facilitates the new approaches to teaching and learning. (Lumby and Briggs, 2002, pp. 56–7)

These strategies to vary teaching were in use for 16–19-year-olds. It is unclear how far they are in use in 14–16 teaching, where the much larger range of subjects, and therefore time pressure, is greater, and where assumptions about the degree of control needed may differ.

As well as influencing teaching approaches, the structure also directs the focus of teaching. Staff in schools seemed to place a low priority on addressing education *outcomes*, that is, young people entering employment, training or further education immediately or in the longer term, or at least to place it much lower than targets concerned with education *outputs*, examination and value-added scores (Lumby et al., 2003b). The focus was embedded through the structure, with staff perceiving that the timetable would not allow much time for supporting the process of choosing a post-16 pathway and a career. Thus, young people who had not much hope of achieving a large number of GCSEs and/or high grades were not able to access greater support in deciding their future route because of the rigidity of the timetable.

As well as efforts to vary the teaching within schools and colleges, options in the location for learning have widened, as discussed in Chapter 4. A sizeable number of young people now spend part of their time away from their main site of education or training, for example, in a college while attending a school, in a workplace while attending college or in a college while employed. The first of these is the most radical change. Research has consistently shown that school pupils in further education colleges value the different environment, particularly the greater freedom, sense of adulthood, and easy relation with tutors. The diminished power distance between them and their teachers and the wider learning community embracing 14 year olds to those of 80 or older is experienced as liberating by many. Equally, the perceived greater vocational relevance motivates their learning (Higham et al., 2004). The much narrower relevance of training in hairdressing or car mechanics challenges the judgement that such programmes are more vocationally relevant than, say, GCSE Mathematics. What young people may be responding to in assigning greater relevance is both a more obvious connection with the world they inhabit and their culture, and also teaching methods which are more activity based. Research in the UK and internationally has identified a preference for more active and participatory styles of learning, though for all the reasons discussed in this section of the chapter, young people may not always get their choice (Hughes, 1997; Lumby, 2001a; Mortimore, 1999).

Technologies

The advent of a wider range of technologies to support learning has opened up possibilities for new ways of supporting learning. The terminology varies, but flexible learning will be used here as encompassing a range of technology-based learning techniques. Flexible learning is championed as increasing learner independence, involvement and therefore motivation. It is also cited as having the potential to shape learning to match individual needs, including focus and pace, much more than previous methods (Bond, 1993). However, the use of new technologies such as web-based learning, resource-based learning, interactive whiteboards and so on are still highly dependent on the skill of the educator designing the learning process. Appending a different name to a learning activity does not in itself change the nature of the learning:

> The names given to learning activities can mean very little. For example, a lesson devoted to 'class teaching' could be organised in a flexible and participative style with input from the teacher nicely punctuated with individual or small group tasks in order to give the students a strong sense of involvement. Conversely a lesson devoted to 'independent study' could be a dreary trudge through a succession of monotonous worksheets which give no scope for decision making or personal contribution. (Temple, 1992, p. 229)

Investigations into the efficacy of resource-based learning, e-learning and so on have discovered, unsurprisingly, that such methods suit and support the learning of some but are a negative experience for others (Briggs, 1999). The use of such methods are much more widespread in post-16 education, partly reflecting a greater confidence in the ability of learners at this age to self-direct, and partly in response to the pressures to cut contact hours due to financial stringency (Thomas, 1995). Staff have noted the synergy of curriculum changes such as the introduction of GNVQs with the wider range of technologies for active learning (Lumby and Briggs, 2002). However, the dominance of the National Curriculum framework and, post-16, the same pressures of time constraints following the advent of Curriculum 2000 have ensured that classroom-based teaching remains the default position for the majority of young people.

Reality check

In answer to the question posed at the commencement of the chapter, how far can we conclude that teaching has changed since 1979? Clearly there have been changes. Staff have worked hard internally to develop and vary teaching practice, and externally to create partnerships with organizations to widen the learning opportunities available. However, schools and colleges are still largely output driven and the dominant experience of young people is still to learn as part of an age group class within a classroom focusing on a discrete subject. The changes brought about by new technologies have brought more changes in post-16 learning, though this is still seen primarily as an adjunct to more traditional forms of teaching. Though examination results have improved at both 16 and 18, there is little evidence that the liberal humanist philosophy, stressing personal and moral development, has gained any ground. Many leave school with little capacity for independent learning (Davenport, 1993). The demands of mass education serving the needs of society and the economy still hold sway, embedded in a structure and teaching practice which is not so very different from that experienced by young people prior to 1979, and perhaps much earlier still than that. Fourteen to nineteen-year-olds today have moved on. Their expectations and preferences are not the same as earlier generations. Their changing needs are reflected to some degree in the developments in teaching, but as suggested by the figures on truancy and exclusion, not yet enough.

Elbaz (1993) explores the concept of an ecological perspective on teaching. He argues against any oversimplistic analysis of a process as complex as teaching, and suggests there is a need to understand and relate the many elements that in concert result in learning. This chapter has suggested that the nature of 14–19-year-olds, their changing expectations and lifestyles are one such element. The culture and community in which learning takes place is another. The range of methods and technologies which can be brought to bear interact with both elements. While the learning experience of many 14–19-year-olds has changed, evidence suggests changes are largely superficial and that a much more radical reshaping of structure is needed, to focus on outcomes and not just outputs, to challenge the tyranny of the atomization of learning into discrete subjects for discrete age groups in time periods which do not relate to learning objectives. Above all, the credentialism which overwhelms many attempts to overhaul teaching and learning must be reconsidered, and it is this issue to which the next chapter turns.

Chapter 7

Teaching and learning: the ritual of assessment

Whose purpose?

The questions surrounding assessment are neatly summarized as concerning 'who is saying what and to whom and for what purposes' (Taylor, 1998, p. 61). Assessment has always been subject to the tensions of differing answers to these questions. Torrance (1993) argues that there have always been, and probably always will be, competing demands between formative assessment, designed to provide information on learners' strengths and weaknesses, and summative assessment, designed to provide an account to a wider constituency of what the learner has achieved, despite the occasional claim that both can be achieved simultaneously (TGAT, 1987). Though this chapter comes after that on teaching and learning, mirroring a logic that assessment should follow from the selected teaching and learning purposes and strategies, this chapter argues that assessment has driven teaching and learning policy and practice since 1979. It will explore the history of dissatisfaction with the assessment system, the drivers of change, and the consequent development of assessment. It will examine how far the ritual of assessment, traditionally used in the UK as an initiation process designed primarily to select and categorize, barring entry to higher education for the majority, may have developed, and what hope remains for its further development.

The drivers of change

As early as 1960, the Crowther Report noted that the examination system resulted not only in subjects which were not examined becoming unvalued, but also learners who were not successful seeming of lesser worth. There have been many expressions of particularly the latter concern, that the system of examining 16 and 18-year-olds excluded many not just from success, but even from participation (see Chapter 4).There has also been consistent dissatisfaction with the other staple of the system, GCE A level which has been subject to some limited change and to the addition of AVCEs as an alternative qualification (Hodgson and Spours, 2003). Apart from the potentially socially divisive nature of the assessment system, educators have also been concerned that it was inadequately linked to supporting learning (Black and William, 1998). However, at national policy level, it is difficult to differentiate educational concerns from those deriving from economic and social objectives. For example, the accreditation of a much higher proportion of young people in education and training up to 18 may be seen as an ambition to increase the life chances of each individual, but also reflects the necessity to ensure that sufficient numbers of people are educated to the level required by the economy. The demands of equity and economic competitiveness slot neatly together. A further driver of change is unashamedly financial as the government sought to respond to concerns expressed by the Audit Commission, and others, of the high cost of examinations, particularly where the drop-out and failure rate is high (Audit Commission/OFSTED, 1993).

The assumed connection between participation and economic success has been challenged in this volume and elsewhere (Keep, 1999; Steedman, 2002; Wolf, 2002). Nevertheless the conviction of the government that there is a tight coupling between mass educational participation and economic success has further embedded the traditional dominance of summative assessment. To allow government to supposedly assess its position in relation to other nations and to how far the national situation has improved, accreditation must be sufficiently frequent, universal and easily communicated. Consequently, reliability must take precedence over validity, that is, giving an account which provides convincing relative positions outweighs the need to incorporate the subtleties of different understandings of what is worth assessing, and what improvement or progress has been achieved by each individual.

This chapter does not provide a detailed history of changes in the assessment system, which were described in Chapter 4, but will look at the effects of the drivers outlined above. Much of the critique of assessment will be relevant throughout the education system, but it is at the 14–19 phase that assessment becomes most intense and is most critical in its impact on lives. Consequently, the chapter goes on to examine the impact of assessment on 14–19-year-olds.

Conceptions of assessment

Assessment, as defined by the Evidence for Policy and Practice Information and Co-ordinating Centre (EPPI Centre) systematic review of the effects of summative assessment 'is a term that covers any activity in which evidence of learning is collected in a planned and systematic way, and is used to make a judgment about learning'. (Assessment and Learning Research Synthesis Group, 2002, p. 6) They further distinguish two types of assessment:

> If the purpose is to help in decisions about how to advance learning and the judgement is about the next steps in learning and how to take them, then the assessment is formative in function. If the purpose is to summarise the learning that had taken place in order to grade, certificate or record progress, then the assessment is summative in function. (Assessment and Learning Research Synthesis Group, 2002, p. 6)

Broadfoot (1998) sees summative assessment as deriving from nineteenth century concerns to find a fair and reliable means of categorizing merit as a prelude to selection. The categories indicated by terms such as 'score' or 'grade' are the dominant elements of the discourse. The underpinning paradigm is scientific and rational. The intended recipient of the assessment is primarily not the learner, but those who may wish to make use of categories in order to offer or refuse opportunities such as employment or education. The multiple audiences for assessment judgements create tensions in devising a system to meet the varied needs. Currently, there is a lack of clarity in how compromise has been reached to meet the different requirements, and at whose cost.

Summative assessment is contrasted with formative assessment, though in fact any summative assessment is the ultimate form of formative assessment, in that it provides feedback which limits and shapes learners' pathways. The results of examinations are taken extremely seriously by learners and teachers as guidance for what learners could and should do next. Despite this, a distinction is made by practitioners and commentators between the two types of assessment. Black and William (1998) in their review of the recent literature on assessment conclude that there is a growing emphasis on formative assessment, largely because of the belief that it is linked more strongly to supporting learning. However, the exact understanding of 'learning' is not always made explicit. The broad definition of formative assessment given above does not indicate the variety of underlying assumptions which relate to different conceptualizations of learning. For example, Black and William (1998) point out that formative assessment is often seen to mean offering learners feedback, which is a term deriving from scientific terminology concerned with electrical circuits. Thus the four elements of feedback are:

- data on the actual level of some measurable attribute
- data on the reference level of that attribute
- a mechanism for comparing the two levels, and generating information about the gap between the two levels
- a mechanism by which the information can be used to alter the gap (Black and William, 1998, p. 33).

This common 'mind the gap' approach may reflect an understanding of the process of learning for which Tunstall (2003, p. 508) uses the metaphor of a copying machine to depict 'a kind of selective, but order-reserving copying machine, with degrees of freedom at the registering, storing and printout points'. He contrasts this with alternative concepts of learning concerning organic growth, where feedback is much more a process of increasing understanding of the whole process of learning and negotiating the creation of knowledge and understanding. Such a concept relates strongly to sociological analyses which seek to understand why learning, even within the same classroom, can be such a different experience for each individual. These two differing approaches reflect, broadly speaking, behaviourist or constructivist theories of learning (Torrance, 1993). The major point is that formative assessment does not in itself imply a single concept or approach to practice but, rather, primarily a function, to improve learning, and a recipient, the learner, both of which differ from summative assessment. The aim to improve learning is related to both short-term goals of increasing achievement and longer-term goals of building learning skills as part of the lifelong learning agenda.

The link to learning rests primarily on two claims for formative assessment, that it empowers learners and that it increases learner motivation, the two of course being related. Torrance (1993) urges some caution in conclusions about how far motivation is improved, pointing out that much of the evidence is self-reported teacher perception. Overall, the literature appears to suggest that motivation can be increased by the use of formative assessment, but that the nature of the process and the context within which it takes place are critical. Given the overwhelming culture which values summative assessment, changing classroom practice to achieve the appropriate context and process is fraught.

The discussion about empowerment is also complex. Claims that formative assessment can empower students rest largely on the belief that it is an essential part of increasing learner autonomy (Wolf, 1998). However, autonomy itself can be conceived in a number of ways, and the often stated central aim to achieve autonomy by transferring responsibility for learning to learners is highly problematic. Analysis of the experience of GNVQs, which were, at least initially, explicitly designed to increase student autonomy, points up the issues. While GNVQ students are more likely than A level students to believe that they control the method of working and pace (Wolf, 1998), the control is within defined boundaries. If, for example, students choose to work too slowly in the view of the teacher, the latter is likely to retake control. 'Students' new found freedoms were highly conditional on their performing as required' (Bates, 1998, p. 20). As well as being subject to teacher control, the outcomes and the method of summative assessment, by portfolio and test, are specified at national level. Thus, the degree to which learners achieve 'autonomy' in GNVQs is questionable. Some question the very notion of learner autonomy:

> The danger of putting the learner at the centre, from whichever perspective we view the model, is that other things are seen as off-centre. This is not to say that we think that the teacher or the technology, for instance, should themselves be at the centre … A model similarly skewed in favour of the learner does not attract anything like the same opprobrium but it may be equally unrealistic, because at many levels at which the purposes of learning are determined the learner is not even present … Somebody must represent the interests of the learner. (Thomas, 1995, p. 6)

Fourteen to nineteen-year-old learners, in their inexperience and vulnerability cannot experience autonomy in any complete sense. The aim is rather one of shifting the balance of control, but retaining the essential role of teachers in the learning and assessment process.

The distinction between summative and formative assessment conceals a range of differing underpinning theory and concept. It is debated often in ritual terms where phrases such as lifelong learning and learner autonomy are used unproblematically, not to get to grips with the real issues in the assessment system, but as a way of concealing the discordance between stated aims, for example empowering students, and the reality of empowering those, employers and universities amongst others, who select. Despite this confusion and obfuscation, the development of assessment since 1979 has had major effects on practice and on the experience of learning.

Summative assessment

Though much of the theory of assessment discussed above relates to the whole age range, there is a cumulative rise in the stakes at 14–19. The increase in frequency of testing with the introduction of Standard Attainment Tests (SATs) at 14, the examination of GCSEs at 16, examination of both 17-year-olds at AS level and 18-year-olds at A2 in Curriculum 2000, and periodic assessment for NVQ units etc. means that the effects of assessment are intensified. The aim to retain young people in school from 14 onwards, in combination with a desire to give a full and accurate account of achievement have also particularly shaped the development of assessment methods. Consequently, assessment at 14–19 is at the forefront of developing systems.

In some ways the development of the summative assessment system for 14–19 year olds might be seen as a success. There has been an increase in participation. Where approximately 60 per cent took GCE O levels and CSEs prior to 1984, well over 90 per cent of 16-year-olds now take one or more GCSEs or GNVQs (DfES, 2003c). The percentage of the relevant age group taking A levels rose from 15 to more than 33 per cent over the last three decades of the twentieth century (Anthony, 1994). The average pass rate at both levels continues to rise, though the variation amongst schools and colleges is still wide. One argument for increasing the frequency of testing is that testing in itself raises achievement, by providing feedback and goals. Certainly, if measured in numbers of 14–19-year-olds achieving accreditation, results would seem to bear out this claim. However, this apparent success has continued to be dogged by persistent concerns about the exclusion of some, the narrowness of achievement recorded and the negative effects on learning. Additionally, the inflation of credential values in itself leads to criticism of their value. Ten GCSEs at A*–C are seen as outstanding where eight were previously. Achieving three As at A level no longer impresses as it did. A spiral ensues where results continue to improve leading to the charge that standards are dropping. At the other end of the achievement spectrum, the failure of some to achieve accreditation may be a deterrent to staying on in education. Young people are not anxious to re-submit themselves to a process which offers humiliation.

Multiple concerns have led to some innovations in assessment. The outcomes- or competencies-based approach was initially introduced with the establishment of the National Council for Vocational Qualifications in 1984. The qualifications offered through the NCVQ, National Vocational Qualifications, were founded on a very different approach and were highly ambitious (Hillier, 1996). Initially aimed at post-16 training, they were based on a process of presenting evidence of various kinds to demonstrate competence against a range of outcomes. The timescale, support for learning (if any) and place of presenting evidence were all unspecified. Qualifications no longer rested on being enrolled in a school or college. Nor did they follow from a prescribed course of study. As a criterion-referenced system, all who wished potentially could succeed, if necessary by development and representation of evidence. The system was therefore designed, though summative, to be 'learner-centred' (Jessup, 1991). It was also intended to produce authentic judgements about skills in action as assessment took place in a real work environment. In essence, NVQs decoupled qualifications from a course of study and an educational environment. However, the competence approach drew a number of criticisms relating to the narrowness of the curriculum, the deprofessionalization of teachers and the lack of concern for learning processes, which have been summarized in Chapter 4. Additionally, the weight of bureaucracy in portfolio assessment and the unreliability of judgements have elicited repeated concern (Smithers, 1994; Wolf, 1998). Despite such criticisms, and the fact that NVQs have remained throughout the period since 1979 a marginal qualification for 14–19 year olds, the influence of the outcomes-based approach on assessment of this age range has been considerable.

The notion of an assessment process based on specified outcomes and comprising scrutiny of a portfolio of evidence was influential and supported the development of other initiatives such as GNVQs and the Record of Achievement (ROA), both of which use portfolios as a central component of assessment. A portfolio can be defined as 'quite simply a pile of paper which may or may not fit into one receptacle' (Wolf, 1998, p. 6). It may also contain videos, photographs and artifacts. The ROA, first piloted in 1984, was an attempt to both capture a wider range of achievement and to incorporate self-assessment and reflection by the learner. As such, it was seen as a challenge to the dominant mechanistic and academic assessment regime. It became mandatory in 1993, following a sea change which required schools to reshape the ROA 'towards the reporting of academic achievements under the national curriculum to parents. The purpose, scope and form of reporting were to be external to the pupil' (Broadfoot, 1998, p. 15). The aspiration to record a wider range of skills and to include a wider range of judges, including the learner, has faltered. The intention of GNVQs is hard to discern, because, as Ecclestone (2000) graphically describes, their evolution has been subject to a maelstrom of political disagreement, compromise and confusion. They mark a midway point between academic education and vocational training, and between conventional written examinations and an outcomes portfolio approach. Though the intention may have been to empower the learner, the net effect has often been a focus on coping strategies to assemble information, and teachers spending anything from five to 26 hours a week viewing portfolios which often comprise 1,000 pieces of paper (Wolf, 1998). Evaluation suggest that at all levels – the learner, the teacher and the verifier – the focus is on the production of evidence, not on learning (Hodgson and Spours, 1997). Just as ROAs reverted towards the dominant assessment approach of written tests, GNVQs also have been subject to a swing to written testing. At the government's insistence, an element of written testing has always been included, and in 2000 became one-third of the process (Ecclestone, 2000).

Despite experimentation with different forms of assessment, the default position of written tests holds strong for 14–19-year-olds. Only for a minority on Modern Apprenticeship or other forms of vocational training, and at the periphery with initiatives such as the ROA, are other approaches evident. The value of qualifications is negotiated within the 'standards' debate in which standards referring to *maintenance of a norm-referenced level of achievement*, and standards referring to *a criterion-referenced level of competence* are sometimes conflated and sometimes set in opposition. Overall, the systematic review of the effects of summative assessment system on the motivation of learners carried out by the EPPI-Centre drew a pessimistic picture of how far assessment is supporting learning. The high weight of evidence they reviewed indicated, amongst other findings, not only the negative effects of summative assessment in SATs and examinations on learners, but also on teachers' practice:

- When passing tests is high stakes, teachers adopt a teaching style which emphasizes transmission teaching of knowledge.
- Repeated practice tests reinforce the low self-image of the lower-achieving students.

- Students are aware of a performance ethos in the classroom and that the tests give only a narrow view of what they can do.
- Students dislike high-stakes tests, show high levels of test anxiety (particularly the girls) and prefer other forms of assessment.
- Feedback on assessments has an important role in determining further learning.
- High-stakes tests can become the rationale for all that is done in classrooms.
- An education system that puts great emphasis on evaluation produces students with strong extrinsic orientation towards grades and social status (adapted from Assessment and Learning Research Synthesis Group, 2002, pp. 9–10).

Though the review also emphasised the critical and positive role of teachers, the overwhelming conclusion is that the summative assessment system has a negative impact on learning.

Formative assessment

The discussion above on the learning theories underlying the use of formative assessment makes it clear that, when it reflects behaviourist theory, formative assessment can amount to not much more than ongoing summative assessment. In order to fulfil its potential to support learning, formative assessment needs to go much further than this. It is potentially:

> Much more than techniques of feedback on progress or processes of reviewing and recording achievement. Instead, it is better conceived as an interactive pedagogy based on constructivist ideas about learning and integrated into a range of learning and support activities ... we should replace the technical terms 'formative' and 'diagnostic' assessment with 'assessment for learning'. (Ecclestone and Pryor, 2003, p. 472)

This phrase is the official term used by the Qualifications and Curriculum Authority (Assessment and Learning Synthesis Group, 2002). Given that such a definition underpins practice, claims are made that formative assessment can significantly improve learning (Black and William, 1998). However, the literature indicates that the nature of feedback is critical and that feedback of the wrong kind can have negative effects on self-esteem and learning (Cameron and Pierce, 1994; Dweck, 1986). In particular, the differential effects of the same approach to feedback on high and low achievers are important. Black and William (1998) draw on the work of Dweck (1986) to summarize the elements of successful use of feedback to support learning:

> The crucial variables appear to be:
> personalization (whether factors are internal or external);
> permanence (whether the factors are stable or unstable);
> specificity (whether the factors are specific and isolated or whether they are global, generalisable and transferable).
>   The clear message from the research and attribution theory ... is that teachers must aim to inculcate in their students the idea that success is due to internal, unstable, specific factors such as effort, rather than on stable general factors such as ability (internal) or whether one is positively regarded by the teacher (external). (Black and William, 1998, p. 35)

The implication is that using formative feedback effectively, as Ecclestone (2000) argues, is not just an intuitive part of good teaching, but needs careful study and attention in its own right. For example, the generally held belief that praising students is part of good teaching, raises their self-esteem and motivation, and therefore improves learning, does not necessarily hold true in giving formative feedback. Counter-intuitively, Cameron and Pierce (1994) found that while praise may raise interest, it has no effect on performance. Further, praise which locates the cause of success in stable personal attributes may lessen the learner's belief in his or her capacity to improve performance. As several commentators point out, the effective use of formative feedback is likely to be highly challenging (Broadfoot, 1998; Ecclestone, 2000).

As well as indicating that feedback must be very carefully handled in the interaction between the individual learner and the teacher, the overall culture within which such interaction takes place is also significant. The dominant culture may easily overwhelm the intended messages given within formative assessment and, if contradictory, negate them. For example, if the overall culture of a school is embedded in structures which locate ability as a prime factor in success, for example through setting or selection, formative indications that effort counts for more are undermined. Similarly, if the focus is primarily on product, examination results, rather than process, learning to learn, then the latter may get short shrift in terms of the priorities of learners, whatever individual teachers attempt.

Radical change then is needed both at classroom and national level. The current 14–19 system subjects teenagers, at the very time when their self-esteem is most fragile, to an intense assessment regime which may challenge or damage the self-esteem of many. The implication is that a move to a constructivist conception of learning and its practical implementation in classroom and workshop practice is required. This will be a long journey from the current position. Teachers' practice is generally at the other end of the spectrum, reflecting the values and techniques of summative assessment and a behaviourist conception of learning. Black and William (1998) draw on the work of Crooks (1998) and Black (1993) to identify the key elements in teachers' current practice in formative assessment. The overall picture was one of weak practice. Key weaknesses were:

- Classroom evaluation practices generally encourage superficial and rote learning, concentrating on recalling isolated details, usually items of knowledge which pupils soon forget.
- The grading function is overemphasized and the learning function under emphasized.
- There is a tendency to use a normative rather than a criterion approach, which emphasizes competition between pupils rather than personal improvement of each (adapted from Black and William, 1998, p. 10).

They point out that the effect of this on weaker pupils is to make them feel they lack ability, and they become demotivated and lose confidence in their capacity to learn.

The response to rectifying this situation has been both to widen the techniques in use and to train teachers. Self and peer review have been added to teachers' feedback, and with some success. In Stefanis's (1994) study of college students, all felt that self-assessment made them think more and 85 per cent felt it helped them learn. Support in developing study skills, group work with purposeful composition of groups to meet the learning task and use of peer assessment have also been added to the range of possible, if not common, techniques for 14–16-year-olds and, more frequently, for 17–19-year-olds. However, the effectiveness of the use of formative assessment, as has been argued in this chapter, rests primarily in the quality of the interaction with staff, and the nature of the culture within which the interaction tales place. There are resource implications, in that teachers need time to provide appropriate feedback. Current resource models make this problematic. While amending or widening the techniques used in teaching have their place (assuming the resource is provided to achieve this), the most critical requirement is a change in the nature of the relationship between teachers and learners and in the thinking of both teachers and the government. At the individual level, the power differential between teacher and learner is a defining parameter of how far the learner can be encouraged to feel able to request feedback and to take responsibility for its use to develop learning. What Black and William (1998, p. 11) term the 'existing symbiosis of mutual dependency between teachers and students' is a rock solid impediment to raising the learner's estimate of how far they are able to understand and control their own learning. When the changing nature of 14–19-year-olds (heightened and growing demand for self-direction, disaffection when adolescent self-esteem is threatened) is added to this general difficulty in the relationship between teacher and learner, both the fundamental necessity and the challenge of adjusting the power relations in the teacher–learner interaction is apparent.

However, it is not just a question of the relationship; thinking must also change. When given the opportunity to control assessment, teachers often resort to the default position of written testing and appear thoroughly wedded to the implied theory and values embedded in the dominant summative and traditional forms of assessment. In this they reflect wider society's attachment to formal examinations as a form of initiation to adulthood, suffered by most adults and so a necessary rite of passage demanded of following generations. The government, too, though rhetorically committed to using assessment to support learning, demonstrate in their policy an ongoing commitment to traditional conventional forms of summative testing, for example, in their changes to the GNVQ balance between portfolios and written tests, and in their reshaping of the Record of Achievement. There is a lack of congruence between the espoused primary commitment to using assessment to support learning and the actions both of practitioners and of policy-makers. And, as always, where such a disjuncture occurs, people take note of what is done, not what is said (Schein, 1997). Teachers and government ministers are locked into a concept of learning which is single-loop thinking, that is, identifying the goal and keeping people on track to achieve it, rather than double-loop thinking, which assumes that the goals themselves are open to negotiation, creation and contestation. The effective use of formative assessment to support learning will require more than just developing an understanding of how it best functions in practice (Black and William, 1998). It will be dependant on a profound shift in culture at individual and structural level.

14–19-year-olds

This chapter has explored the values and practice of practitioners and policy-makers but has as yet only touched on those of 14–19-year-olds themselves and how they may view the assessment regime to which they are subject. Much evidence suggests that many of them do not share the attitude to education of teachers, which both teachers and policy makers wish to inculcate. For many, education and assessment are not ends in themselves and not of primary or even of much importance relative to other priorities (De Pear, 1997; Lumby and Briggs, 2002; Morris et al., 1999). Education is in competition with other activities such as part-time work and the high-priority activity of a social life and relationships. Adolescents also may constitutionally not wish to expend effort, if it can be avoided. Consequently, the watershed of age 14 sees learners engaging with education in a context which is qualitatively different to that which went before. Young people have choices to act independently in undertaking paid work. They may also increasingly seek a degree of independence from their families, particularly where relationships may range from poor to physically threatening. The number of young people living outside the family in their own accommodation is rising, and is matched by informal independence where individuals may be seen only rarely in their family home, staying with friends or on the streets as an alternative.

For many, education is a process of getting by, of surviving, of doing the minimum. For others it may be a question of total avoidance, as the experience of perceived failure and oppositional relationships with teaching staff create an environment perceived as uninviting and even hostile in schools and colleges. In summary, work avoidance, fear or simple lack of interest may alienate young people from the learning process generally and from educational organizations in particular. Some, of course, have different attitudes, enjoy learning, are committed to it and see it as a high priority. However, if there is a spectrum from disaffection to deep commitment, the latter is peopled by a minority, the 'boffs'. There is, though, a counter-force. Young people are credential conscious, see the worth of qualifications in an instrumental sense and are acutely aware of the differential status and prestige accorded to different awards and different institutions (Lumby and Wilson, 2003). If they believe they can achieve what they see as having currency, they will attempt it. Qualifications matter to them.

How, then, does this range of context factors in the attitudes of 14–19-year-olds relate to assessment? If increasing autonomy is a prerequisite to lifelong success in the twenty-first century, then the independence of the learner must be taken as serious and real, and not just a rhetorical goal. If this is the case, and 14–19-year-olds may not wish to engage with learning, not because they are afraid, or alienated, but because they do not place it as a high priority, how far can that choice be allowed? If young people are interested only in a narrow range of areas, how far must they be forced to be assessed in a wider range of subjects? The orientation of many 14–19-year-olds calls into question the whole edifice of a wide 14–16 National Curriculum and the ongoing desire to widen study post-16. Secondly, if young people want to get by, to do the minimum, to work smarter, should this be embraced rather than resisted? The trend in the UK is to work ever harder for ever longer hours. In terms of lifelong learning habits, perhaps the desire to limit effort, to hold a social and personal life in balance is to be encouraged as showing the way for the future. The alternative endless exhortation to work harder, deriving from nineteenth-century values and society, may be simply out of date. The upshot may be that practitioners and policy-makers in stressing ever harder work, ever more credentials, are simply far behind. They are basing their decisions and practice on a rapidly disappearing world. Young people may be pointing the direction for the future. Such suggestions may be seen as iconoclastic or even absurd, but they point up the illogic of trying to develop the wish and capacity to learn by the imposition of alien values.

The argument in response is that the economy needs well-qualified people. There is a much stronger argument that it needs people who can learn, and currently assessment appears to be a ritual embedding the myth that tests and credentials provide evidence of learning. Ritual activity may perpetuate activities which people believe erroneously to have certain effects, but which make all *feel* they are doing the right thing. Sacrificing to the gods will change the weather, divert enemies, give bumper crops. From this perspective, the ritual of assessment and awarding credentials makes us *believe* we will have a society better able to adjust to the demands of this century. In fact, as the evidence reviewed here shows, assessment is only loosely connected to learning and may actually be preventing it. It is the twenty-first century equivalent of sacrificing a goat.

Reality check

At the time of writing, a review group headed by Tomlinson is considering the future of 14–19 education. The Green Paper which preceded it focused largely on qualifications (DfES, 2002) and the proposal of the review group to date that has drawn most interest and taken centre stage is the possibility of a UK baccalaureate. Summative assessment and qualifications, as ever, overwhelm interest in developing learning and drive development of the curriculum. The response to both the Green Paper and the review group proposal note that there is little likely to challenge the traditional values and assumptions (DfES, 2002). The response suggests, in common with this chapter, that wholesale change, for example in deconstructing the competitive climate so teachers can focus on learning not league tables, is needed. At this point in time there seems little hope of such a radical change. Nevertheless, the vision of what assessment could achieve refuses to die. The evidence mounting on the negative affects of the credentialism climate (Assessment and Learning Research Synthesis Group, 2002) may persuade, at the least, of the need for some lessening of the obsession with targets, league tables and ubiquitous summative assessment.

Chapter 8

Choices, transitions and 14–19 pathways

Fourteen to nineteen is one of the most important transition periods in people's lives. Choosing pathways, progression to further and/or higher education, and choosing careers have a high profile during this formative period. Choice lies at the heart of the whole 14–19 system, just as it has become one of the watchwords of education across much of the developed world. A realignment of the aims of education that places the learners, their wants and their needs at the focus of the system has been a strong metatrend (Levin, 2003). Reflecting this trend, the 14–19 system is modelled to be driven by the choices of young people, which in turn shape the choices made by schools, colleges and training organizations about what, where and how they offer education and training. Yet, at the same time, the choices of young people are not the most significant part of the system, for it is the choices of successive governments about the economic, social and political aims of education and training that frame and shape the system. Indeed, the very introduction of choice-based market systems is itself the choice of government!

This chapter explores how young people perceive the options, assign them value and choose between them. At 14, young people are at the end of Key Stage 3 in secondary education. While the minimum school-leaving age is still two years away, their general broad-based education is close to completion as they begin to make choices that shape their future pathways. Choices of subject for Key Stage 4 begin to represent specialization and, traditionally, a long-term commitment towards either academic or vocational pathways. At 16 the choices are more fundamental, with the first opportunity officially to leave education, and yet more choices of pathway, institution and potential destination. Choice then becomes continuous, with annual cycles of assessment to drive choice, pressure from within schools and colleges (and society) to make choices for the period beyond 18, and recurring opportunities to leave education. By 18 most of the dies have been cast. Forty per cent of young people have entered higher education, most of the rest are in employment with training, and some 20 per cent are in jobs without training or fall into the NEET category. The future direction for most has been largely formed by the time they reach their nineteenth birthday. The 14–19 phase, therefore, represents the transition from school to higher education or from school to employment and, most importantly, from child to adult and from schoolchild to participant in the labour market.

If choice is the driving force, then understanding the processes of choice and the way in which they shape and/or respond to the market is essential for all stakeholders. In terms of policy development it is critical to know how choice will operate. For the government, for example, the introduction of innovations such as Curriculum 2000 or Modern Apprenticeships requires, in theory, an understanding of how young people will respond to the changing environment, and what specific actions might encourage the positive take-up of such innovation. In reality, of course, choice policies were introduced on the basis of assumptions about how they might operate in the quasi-markets of education. It is only later that the evidence of how young people and organizations have actually responded to the markets has been measured and analysed (Gorard, Fitz and Taylor, 2003).

For schools and colleges, understanding choice is important from two perspectives. First, each institution has responsibility for delivering the strategy and policy of government in a way that makes it 'work'. This can only be achieved where the institution knows very well both the generic ways in which choice operates and also how their own local markets operate. Recognition that every local micro-market is in some way unique is essential (Gewirtz et al., 1995). Secondly, though, schools and colleges have a direct responsibility for shaping choice, in that they are charged with providing effective guidance and support for young people as they navigate the 14–19 landscape. Understanding how and why and when young people make choices is important in providing that support. It is also important from an entirely selfish perspective in that all education and training organizations operate in a competitive market, and being able to influence choice is important to institutional well-being and, even, survival.

For young people, too, having some understanding of choice is helpful. The landscape they have to navigate is complex and, for many, unclear. The challenge this poses has stimulated the government to promote effective information and guidance for young people through the

Connexions service. Having a good understanding of what young people might need to consider and also of how other stakeholders may be able to help choice or may be seeking to influence choice will certainly be supportive. Learning to choose and learning the skills of decision-making are important life skills for young people. Just as important, though, is that all players in the educational and training system understand the connection between choice and the wider issues of late teenage lifestyle priorities, personal development and culture. While choice is the main focus of the education service, for many young people it is only a small part of their life. The rituals of choosing, of applications, interviews, of choice itself are designed by the education system on behalf of society. For many young people these rituals represent a threat, a challenge to self-esteem and peer esteem and an invitation to be seen to fail the selection process. Furthermore, that choice process is made more confusing and contradictory by the range and complexity of choice. We consider below how this process operates.

The nature of choice

Choice in the 14–19 arena must be considered in the context of broader models of choice in education and training. Our understanding of choice has changed fundamentally during the last decade as a result of both our observation of educational choice in action and the evidence from research. The traditional view (for example, Janis and Mann, 1977) was that choice is a rational, logical process that involves evaluating a number of alternatives to enable a single choice to emerge. Evidence from a vigilant process of information collection would shape choice, and that choice was seen as a clear single act. In such circumstances, influencing choice is achievable simply by providing the right information at the right time. In the context of such rationality, early research (for example, Stillman and Maychell, 1986) sought to identify factors that influence choice (for example, location, parents) and identify their relative importance. However, more recent research has been highly critical of such views of choice, in that focusing on individuals' priorities from lists of choice factors *presumes* that choice is rational (Gewirtz et al., 1995).

Three groups of choice models have emerged from research. Structuralist models (for example, Gambetta, 1996) present choice as resulting from institutional, cultural or economic constraints over which young people have no choice. In a sense the hidden hand of 'structuralist' views means that young people may not be making real decisions at all, since their pathways and destinations can be predicted from their context and environment. The key contention against such models is that many young people do make decisions that are outside the expected outcomes for their social group or cultural heritage.

Economic, or human capital, models (for example, Becker, 1975) assume that choice is made on estimations (formal or informal) by young people of the relative economic return from different choices. While it is recognized that this is an important component of choice, a significant issue is that economic benefits from education and training are long term and for many young people long-term views are problematic.

The third group of models is based on the importance of personality and subjective judgement, and the view that 'choice is a rational process that is constrained by a realistic perception of opportunities and shaped by individual personality' (Payne, 2002, p. 13). Hemsley-Brown (1999) has shown, for example, that while young people often give rational and utilitarian reasons for their choices, they have in fact been filtered through layers of preconceptions arising from the influences of family background, culture and the individual's life history. Hodkinson and Sparkes (1997) have developed the concept of a 'learning career', for example, which suggests that the value young people attribute to education or training changes in response to influences both within their school/college and outside in their personal lives, and that learning may fluctuate between possessing high and low value over relatively short periods of time.

Foskett and Hemsley-Brown (2001) have brought together the key elements of the groups of models into a single integrated model that tries to show the complexity of the choice process (Figure 8.1). The model shows the processes that are all occurring simultaneously that constitute 'choice'. The context represents the environment in which choice is taking place, and comprises the macro-environment of the social, economic and political world, and the directly experienced environments of the individual chooser. This direct environment comprises the home, the social world they inhabit (which includes their socio-economic group or ethnicity), their institutional environment (the school or college they attend) and the lived environment of their day-to-day lives. Young people take a view of this world that reflects their own direct perceptions and also the perceptions that have been passed to them through the filters of parental, teacher or peer views and opinions. These perceptions are then subject to a wide range of internal psychological processes by the chooser, including, for example, their lifestyle ambitions and the impact they believe particular choices may have on their self-esteem or their status in the eyes of their peers. Out of this, at any one moment is a view (or choice) of what they would wish to do in terms of career, college, programme and so on. It must be stressed that all these processes are simultaneous and dynamic, and so are subject to constant revision and change. Choice is therefore a momentary balance between these processes, and the actual choice that a young person makes will depend on their precise views and perceptions at the moment that decision is required from them.

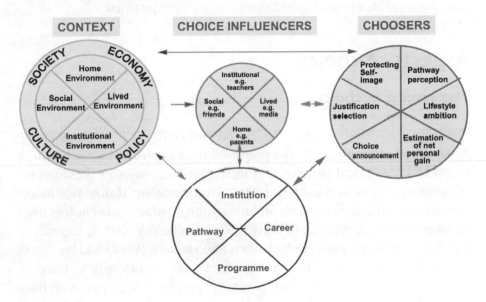

Figure 8.1
A generic model of young people's choice (after Foskett and Hemsley-Brown, 2001)

From this model we can stress a number of key components of 'choice'. First, choice is an expression of the balance of elements in the model at a particular moment. Secondly, while choice is not strictly rational, it is also not irrational or random, and is what Hodkinson and Sparkes (1997) term 'pragmatic rationality'. As Foskett et al. (2004, p. 5) indicate: 'Choices ... will reflect some active process by the chooser, but that process will have been based on partial evidence, perception and circumstance rather than any rational, comprehensive and objective search for, and weighing of, evidence.' Thirdly, the importance of perception and individuality cannot be overestimated. There is no deterministic link between a particular set of circumstances and an inevitable single choice, for individuals perceive the circumstances and contexts in highly individual ways. Fourthly, lifestyle perceptions and issues of style and fashionability are important (Foskett et al., 2003). 'Decisions' are often made on the basis of the lifestyle that will accrue, in the short term or long term, from that decision rather than on the basis of the job or course itself. Particular courses, careers or institutions, for example, swing in and out of fashion over a period of time with particular social groups. Finally, the promotion of self-esteem for individuals and the pressure to achieve peer approval are important in shaping both choices and the ways in which those choices are publicly justified.

Aspects of choice

The timing of choice

The initial provision of careers education and guidance (CEG) is made by most schools during year 10 as a preparation for choice at 16. Such timing is rooted in historical patterns and in the limited resources provided for information advice and guidance (IAG). Unfortunately, it does not reflect current understanding of when and how young people *make* choices (that is, form choice) as opposed to when they *take* choices (that is, commit to a particular choice). Research by Foskett and Hesketh (1997) and Foskett et al. (2004) confirms that most young people start consciously to think of choices post-16 when they are in year 9, and that 5–10 per cent have started before then. Furthermore, girls tend to start the process earlier than boys, so that fewer girls are 'undecided' by the end of year 11, and those opting for academic pathways have settled on their choice earlier than those opting for vocational pathways. Importantly, research on career perceptions and choice (Foskett and Hemsley-Brown, 2001) suggests that decisions to exclude particular pathways and careers is made by many pupils prior to leaving primary school, so the processes emerging consciously at 14 are taking place in a context of constrained choice.

If 14–19 is recognized as the period of development from school pupil in basic education to the young person with a relatively clearly defined education/training/career direction, then IAG (and CEG) must begin earlier than age 14. Information advice and guidance within the 14–19 period must focus much more on steering the course and enabling choice of alternative direction rather than being the first point of choice. Engaging young people in thinking about 14–19 transitions earlier may militate against some of the tensions and concerns that currently emerge for many about the choices they face. The implications of this for those providing IAG are substantial, and LSCs, Connexions services and schools and colleges will need to reflect on their engagement with much younger pupils in school if they are to influence choice at 14, 16 or beyond.

The role of schools

The role of schools in influencing choice is important, whether the school provides for 14–16 or 14–19. Young people report that their experiences in school have helped shape their choosing (for example, Foskett and Hesketh, 1997). More importantly, though, Paterson and Raffe (1995) and Ferguson and Unwin (1996) have shown that even after taking account of the influence of GCSE results and socio-economic context there are substantial differences between schools in both post-16 participation rates and the patterns of pathway choices. There would seem to be, therefore, unique facets of a school's organization, structure or culture that promote or dissuade young people from particular pathways through 14–19. Three aspects of this appear to be significant.

First, through contact with teachers through from primary school into secondary education, young people are exposed to the views, attitudes and values of the school and its staff. These views are all-pervasive, so that, for example, the emphasis on academic pathways and progression on to, ultimately, higher education, that characterizes some schools in 'middle-class' suburban areas reinforces and promotes existing cultures emanating from home. Hemsley-Brown (1999) has shown, for example, how the predominance of choice of academic pathways post-16 is linked strongly to the academic ethos of the pre-16 school.

Secondly, individual teachers carry the responsibility as key informal sources of labour market and careers knowledge. However, their own knowledge is highly constrained and limited by their own personal experience, so there is a risk of misinformation or at least cultural replication by teachers whose own experience is of academic pathways (Foskett and Hemsley-Brown, 1999).

Thirdly, careers guidance is important to balance existing attitudes and knowledge of young people as they shape their choices, particularly amongst young people whose home background has limited knowledge and understanding of post-16 education and training. While CEG provided by Connexions services can approximate to independent guidance, resource constraints mean that for many young people the CEG they receive is dominantly provided by careers teachers in schools, which will itself reflect the priorities of the teachers and the school. One study of choice of Modern Apprenticeships in London schools (Hemsley-Brown and Foskett, 2000) showed, for example, that the key factor in take-up of MAs was not GCSE grades but the knowledge of MAs of the careers teacher and the emphasis placed on MAs by the school.

A recent study of the influence of schools on choice at 16 (Foskett et al., 2004) has clarified some of the ways schools exercise this influence. The most significant patterns that emerge are:

- The influence of the school reflects six factors – school type; the nature of the careers programme within the school; the socio-economic status (ses) of the school's catchment; the culture and ethos of the school; the influence of teachers; the organization of the curriculum
- Overall knowledge of post-16 options is greatest amongst young people who are attending a school with its own sixth form – but knowledge of non-academic pathways is greatest amongst those attending schools without their own sixth form
- School is a less important influence on choice than parents for those young people opting for a post-16 academic pathway, but for young people from lower socio-economic backgrounds the school is a very important influence.

From the analysis of the ways in which this influence operates Foskett et al. (2004) have identified four broad forms of school organizational and leadership style that seem to generate distinct outcomes in terms of choice.

1. A *school-focused* culture is one in which the school is primarily concerned with its own institutional achievements and status, usually focused on high pupil achievement as measured in academic terms – high GCSE and A level results and a concern only for progression to higher education. Such schools tend to have their own sixth form and are usually in high ses localities. They have an assumption that pupils will stay in the school for post-16 education, and as a result have minimal connection with mediating agencies (for example, Connexions) or information on alternative post-16 pathways.

2. A *student-centred* school is driven by its pupils' needs and places a strong emphasis on pupils finding the pathway most suited to their individual needs. Such schools use a rich network of information, guidance and advice from a wide range of sources and mediating agencies, and have a strong structure of support throughout the school to support pupils in decision-making. Such schools typically do not have their own sixth form and serve lower ses localities.

3. *Functional/administrative-focused* schools emphasize the place of procedures and systems. In such schools CEG is channelled through a narrow range of routes and is in effect delegated to the careers or Connexions service. With the pathways in place the school assumes that pupils will be receiving appropriate support, and such schools are typically focused on other aspects of pre-16 education, such as special needs or Key Stage 3 curriculum.

4. The fourth form of school has a *strategic/policy* orientation, although in many ways this is simply a sub-form of the student-centred school. Its distinctive nature is a rapid and dynamic responsiveness to changing external policy and organizational changes. Government initiatives, for example, are implemented quite quickly, and the school is eager to respond to partnership or developmental initiatives.

The four models represent extreme positions, and most schools show some combination of elements within their profile. With time, schools can move between the types. Clearly each type of school meets the need for IAG in different ways, reflecting the culture, history and environment of the school, and will meet the needs of some pupils more effectively than others.

The role of colleges and post-16 providers

Over 50 per cent of young people leave school at 16 to pursue a post-16 pathway elsewhere, usually in a sixth form college or an FE college. For those who do not leave their school there has still been the option to leave, and many will at least have considered this option. All post-16 providers are in competition with each other, and as a result it is clear that young people will be exposed to their promotional activities.

A number of studies have considered the role of post-16 providers in shaping choice (Foskett and Hesketh, 1997; Foskett et al., 2004; Hemsley-Brown, 1999; Hodkinson and Sparkes, 1997; Nicholls, 1994). This research shows that a combination of inertia, staying with friends, and a view that an academic school sixth form is the most likely guarantor of entry to HE, is a motivation for most young people pursuing an academic pathway to opt to stay in their school sixth form, if it has one. For those pursuing vocational pathways, or in localities where post-16 colleges are the main providers, then choice is driven strongly by the availability of a course of choice, allegiances with friends, academic reputation and accessibility. Overall, for those choosing either academic or mixed academic/vocational pathways the view that entry to HE is the ultimate goal means that young people choose an institution and programme that optimizes their chance of achieving this goal. For those pursuing vocational programmes, peer conformity, accessibility and programme availability are the main drivers of 'choice'.

A key issue is the availability and reliability of information for young people. Nicholls (1994) identified the issue of young people in schools not being exposed to post-16 information from other providers as a mechanism for encouraging them to choose to stay in school, and this problem clearly persists (Foskett et al., 2004). Hemsley-Brown (1999) has shown how the information provided by colleges is important in the choice process, but questions its accuracy. Gleeson (1996) and Watts and Young (1997) have identified how the priority for recruitment by colleges and the strength of internal markets means that information both at college level and at course level may not be provided entirely in the young person's interests. Guidance in 11–16 schools about post-16 choice may be more objective than that in 11–18 schools, as may that provided by independent organizations such as Connexions. But the range of choices and the detail of each potential option is such an information jungle that young people will still have to rely on college information to support their choice-making.

The role of parents

Young people's choice is inevitably influenced, at least implicitly, by parents, although few 14–19 year olds will admit it! As Foskett and Hemsley-Brown (2001, pp. 108–9) suggest:

The decisions young people make are made within frames of reference defined, sometimes explicitly but more frequently implicitly, by their parents ... The final placing of the choice boundaries may only emerge after extensive negotiation between pupils and parents, and the acknowledgement of the role of parents by young people ... may be very limited, as a way of emphasising their own independence.

Ball et al. (2001) have suggested that parental influence on choice is directly proportional to parental level of education. This has been confirmed by Foskett et al. (2004) who show that parents are a more important influence than schools in high ses localities, but that the opposite is true in low ses localities. The commitment of most schools to raising levels of progression means that they recognize that it is with young people from backgrounds with no tradition of 'staying on' beyond 16 that they can play the most significant role. As one headteacher in a low ses school has said:

These young people come from families where nobody has ever studied after 16 except on the job. So their experience of that world is very limited (and) ... for a lot of these young people there isn't encouragement at home. In fact for some of them there may well be discouragement from staying on. (Headteacher, quoted in Foskett et al., 2004, p. 23)

The role of peers

We have identified that an important element in choosing 14–19 pathways is the development of self-esteem, and that friends' choices and social context are important in the choices an individual will make (Ball et al., 2001; Foskett and Hemsley-Brown, 2001). This social context of choice has two distinct meanings. In general terms it describes the broad social and cultural environment of the individual and their family. Social context has a second meaning (Ball et al., 2001), though, since it also encompasses the social and leisure life of an individual. It is in this context that pressures to establish or preserve self-esteem and to make decisions that support group identity are found. The significance of 'lifestyle' in the development of personal image has been identified by Foskett and Hemsley-Brown (2001), and lifestyle is intimately involved with social relations and the establishment and maintenance of social status. Young people bring together their pre-conceptions of careers, pathways, courses and institutions with the pursuit of a choice that will secure social approval in terms of maintaining self-esteem and peer group acceptance. The importance of choosing institutions and programmes that attract 'people like me' or 'people like I aspire to be' is a key element in the choice process. Matching choices, too, to the choices of friends and peers protects group identity and bolsters self-esteem.

Foskett et al., (2003) have examined this in the context of choice in their West London study, and have highlighted the notion of fashionability as a component of choice. Fashionability in this context is seen as the primacy of particular choices on the basis of their perceived acceptability to specific social groups, where that primacy is based on subjective judgements rather than, necessarily, objective measures of value. Choice that reflects fashion will be associated with establishing membership of a social group and of achieving acceptability or enhanced status in that group. It may also indicate rejection of alternative social values or social groups. What is fashionable is often ephemeral and may change, but once fashionable choice patterns become established, positive feedback processes may lead to substantial reinforcement of those patterns.

Within the West London study a number of aspects of fashion in post-16 choice emerged from the data. First, the fashionability of progression through FE to HE was clearly established across a wide range of socio-economic and ethnic groups. Secondly, course choice reflected clear patterns of fashionability. Between school and university, the aim is to be engaged in, at best, a fashionable course, or at least an acceptable course. Consequently, young people may choose a course that is of doubtful suitability in order to meet street credibility criteria amongst their friends (see, for example, Thomas et al., 2002). At the time of the study, for example, young people, careers advisers and institutions all identified the fashionability of courses in media and performance art. Thirdly, choice of institution is strongly influenced by fashion and current trends. In part this is related to the provision of courses that are currently fashionable, with, for example, those colleges providing media and performance arts courses and having positive reputations experiencing strong demand. Additionally, though, particular institutions were seen as popular with particular groups, either because they were familiar and were consequently secure, or because they were new and removed from areas or institutions with perceived poor reputations. Some courses and providers were seen as 'fashionable' and so exerted an attraction that was weakly related to rational choice. Fourth, the choice of future career reflected a relatively limited range of fields, which in turn seemed to be driven by peer acceptability and the fashionability of particular careers. Certain areas were disproportionately represented, notably the fields of computing, sport, law, and hair and beauty.

Understanding young people's choice processes, therefore, must take into account the culture and society that they are part of and the issues of peer pressure, self-esteem and fashionability. Since these are dynamic arenas, the challenge for schools, colleges and training organizations to keep abreast of change is a significant one.

Reality check

Amongst the many arguments for viewing 14–19 as a coherent sector is that it represents the most dynamic period of choice in young people's lives. For the young person passing through the 14–19 phase their experience is one of the continuous presence of choice and pressure to be shaping and making choices. Moments of choice are required at 14, 16, 17 and 18, but the times between are periods in which those choices form and develop and in which some choices can still be made. Additionally, each choice then defines some of the constraints of subsequent choices.

But choice raises a number of fundamental policy issues. First, it is perhaps ironic that the very markets that create the choices available to young people function to constrain or distort the availability of objective information and guidance. At the time young people are faced with complex and challenging choices they face a promotional environment that is hard to navigate through, and there is a real danger that vested interests will outweigh the need for objectivity. While young people recognize that they have become consumers of education and training, they are by virtue of their age relatively unsophisticated in their consumer skills. While services such as Connexions seek to help with this, they may be perceived as simply yet another part of the supply side that may be seeking to deliver on somebody else's agenda.

Secondly, choice favours those with significant cultural capital. Dealing with instability and lack of clarity is easiest for those young people where the range of choices to be made is small, and this tends to be those who from an early stage have decided to pursue an academic pathway towards higher education. Young people from high ses backgrounds in schools focused on academic achievement are those least likely to be troubled by choice, and yet they are the individuals probably best equipped with the cultural capital to handle ambiguity and complexity. For those with no family tradition of FE or HE, in a low ses environment, with pressures to choose across the vocational/academic/training spectrum, the choices are hardest yet the cultural capital is least.

Thirdly, it is important to recognize that education and training choices are only part of the world that 14–19-year-olds experience, and it is essential to understand choice in that context. For many young people their life experience is constructed from their lifestyle, with its component elements of friendship, social life, social activities and part-time jobs – what Wyn and Dwyer (1999) term 'multiple commitments'. Decisions to participate in or drop out of education or training may be a secondary consequence, almost a by-product, of a range of these other life experiences. What this means is that we cannot see education/training 14–19 in isolation from other aspects of young people's lives. There is a need to connect with, for example, health services for young people, the youth work services and key players in the part-time labour markets that young people inhabit if we are to understand choice and the impact of 14–19 education and training policies.

From this analysis it is clear that choice is by no means equally available to all young people, nor is it always inherently 'a good thing'. For many it is a source of pressure and instability and the mechanisms by which the government and society ensure social reproduction while passing the responsibility down to the young people themselves. We return in Chapter 12 to considering how far choice is a virtue or a problem for young people and how far its dominance and profile in 14–19 is appropriate.

PART 3

LEADING TEACHING AND LEARNING

Chapter 9

Paying for learning: resourcing the system

Reformation

Previous chapters have reviewed the cascade of change in policy and practice at national, regional, LEA and school/college levels. This chapter offers a broad review of how we have paid for the changes in both senses of the word. The period has been marked by experimentation on how to widen and vary the sources and methods of distributing funds, and the incentives/pressures to influence how funds are accessed and used. While much of the policy that has developed relates to schools and colleges generally, the particular focus of the chapter is how far 14–19 education in particular has influenced the development of funding, and the consequent impact on 14–19 teaching and learning.

The 14–19 phase has indeed placed particular imperatives on the development of funding systems. The period since 1979 has seen a global trend to increase the numbers of young people staying on in education or training, to raise the level of qualification they achieve and to find ways of paying for the increased costs other than through large rises in taxes (Foskett and Lumby, 2003). Resourcing the 'massification' of education (Hodgson and Spours, 2003) while minimizing additional expenditure has led to a number of effects:

1. *Widening the sources of funds.* The UK has not moved as far as China, where schools run unrelated business activities such as factories to make profit (Fouts and Chan, 1997), or countries such as South Africa where even the poor must pay a fee towards their children's education. It has however experimented with changes which encourage both individuals and particularly industry to contribute more to education and training costs. While, technically, education for 14–19-year-olds remains free at the point of delivery, individual

learners and parents increasingly make an essential contribution to the budget.

2. *Financial incentives to reward success.* The market or quasi-market introduced into education was designed to ensure resources were channelled towards those organizations achieving success – understood as increasing enrolment, retention and achievement – thereby establishing a virtuous circle of attracting funds through an increased roll and/or sponsors.

3. *Ensuring best use of the funds available.* A technical rationalist approach has been promoted as leading to the 'best' use of resources to improve outcomes (Levačić and Glover, 1997). While the understanding and implementation of such concepts as efficiency, cost-effectiveness and value for money may be uncertain or ambiguous, pressure to adopt a new culture of cost awareness and cost control has been embedded through a number of mechanisms, such as the OFSTED requirement to comment on the management of resources.

Various assumptions underpin the changes. First, it is assumed that resources matter. As Levačić and Vignoles (2002) point out, the evidence for a causal relationship between outcomes and resource levels is very uncertain. Nevertheless, players continue to argue that both the level of resource and its means of distribution critically affect the quality of education (West and Pennel, 2000). Secondly, it is assumed that a rational approach to the use of resources in schools will lead to school improvement (Levačić and Glover, 1997). The edifice of information management, financial planning, strategic and development plans all rest on the belief that objective, non-partisan and rational processes to manage resources are possible and will lead to optimum outcomes. Thirdly, the government assumes that educators require control, sometimes directly, sometimes indirectly, and resources are a critical tool for control. The attaching of resource to particular actions, such as increasing the roll, or to particular activities, through the ubiquitous bidding for ring-fenced funds, is evidence of the belief at national and regional government level that educators must be influenced, guided and controlled.

From 1979 to 1988, funds for education were controlled largely through local education authorities which typically used a historic and negotiation-driven approach to setting school and college budgets. A fault line occurred in the late 1980s with the introduction of Local Management of Schools, whereby schools were enabled to manage a budget which was the result of an authority-wide formula relating to the number and nature of learners in each school. The relative financial independence of schools and colleges was confirmed in the 1988 Education Reform Act. College budgets were entirely taken from LEAs by incorporation in 1993. Schools and colleges therefore entered what was largely seen as a new era of independence. The degree to which that independence was real or illusory is still in question. This chapter considers in more detail the widening of sources of funds, experimentation with their distribution, the promotion of rational approaches to resource management, the effects on educational organizations and, finally, the impact on 14–19 learning.

Sources and distribution of funds

The widening of sources of funds to support education has been achieved at both the individual and system levels. The greater degree of self-management and a perceived shortfall in government funds available to support education has unlocked the entrepreneurialism of many in education (Stewart et al., 2004). This impetus has been encouraged by the government, anxious to spread the funding load. Schools have consequently engaged in a range of fund-raising activities. Many of these activities pre-date the 1980s. However, the range and particularly the scale have increased. Such fund-raising events raised £60 million for schools in 2003 (Lepkowska, 2004). However, a more fundamental change is the, in effect, creeping privatization of schools, where parents are requested to make regular donations which may be used not just for 'extras', but to cover the cost of basics such as textbooks and teachers' salaries. Parents now contribute more than £200 million annually to school budgets as well as paying considerable sums to equip their child with necessaries such as stationery and so on (Lepkowska, 2004). Schools may be dependent on parental donations and fund-raising activities to balance the budget. Colleges' ability to offer full-cost training to business and industry allows them to achieve a much higher percentage of their budget from non-government sources. Their more extensive facilities also offer greater opportunities for income generation through lettings and services to the community.

There are, then, a range of entrepreneurial and quasi-commercial activities to generate income undertaken at the *organization* level. The government has also attempted to embed a wider range of sources of funding at the *system* level. The introduction of city technology colleges, and more latterly specialist, schools established a process whereby achievement of funding from industry is a prerequisite for accessing funds from the government. Though CTCs did not achieve the finañcial outcomes anticipated, with only about 20 per cent of capital funds provided by sponsors (Walford, 2000), the principal of shared responsibility for funding was established. While only 15 CTCs were founded, at the time of writing there are nearly 2,000 specialist schools (DfES, 2004a), 54 per cent of all secondary schools and with 1.5 million learners. Consequently, private funding is now established as part of the resourcing of over half of secondary schools.

The principle of sharing investment and reward with industry has also been promoted through the Private Funding Initiative (PFI). The latter was conceived not only as a means of broadening the sources of income to support education, but also 'to introduce skills, ideas and management practices from the private sector' (Shepherd, 1994, p. 1). Rebadged as Public Private Partnerships (PPPs) in 1998, the initiative has led to a relatively small number of collaborative projects primarily related to capital developments (DfEE, nd).

Nevertheless, the source of the majority of funds for both schools and colleges remains the government, and education is still largely supported from taxes raised at local or national level. The income-raising activities described above address the issue of *quantum*. The method of *distribution*, rather than the quantum, has had equally significant effects on the values and practice within schools and colleges.

Distribution of funds

Government funds for 14–19 education are distributed in broad terms through the application of formulae and through offering sources of 'extra' funding to be accessed by a bidding process. Schools receive funds for 14–16 education through their LEA by means of formulae which are complex and contested (West and Pennel, 2000). Post-16 education and training since 1993 has enjoyed funds disbursed by the FEFC, and since 2001, the Local Learning and Skills Councils through formulae which reward recruitment, retention and achievement (Felstead and Unwin, 2001; Lumby, 1996). The formulae make use of proxies for disadvantage such as number of free school meals, number of lone-parent families, or award additional funds on the basis of location, for example, postcodes of learners seen as indicating disadvantage.

One of the major problems in achieving coherence in 14–19 education is, therefore, that the system of funding differs pre- and post-16. Pre-16, the funds are disbursed via LEAs. Post-16 they are disbursed by LLSCs and, although learner numbers and profile are part of the equation, the achievement of accredited outcomes is also rewarded. The latter output-related funding (ORF), whether attached to achieving qualifications or, in work-based learning, employment has had a particularly significant influence on the teaching and learning experience. In the case of schools, the majority of learners who enrol at Key Stage 3 will stay on the roll until 16. Post-16, in sixth forms and colleges and work-based learning, retention is much more challenging. The effects of funding attached to the learner and to the learner's retention and achievement are therefore more acute post-16. Nevertheless, when numbers count, attracting and retaining learners is key to survival both in schools and in colleges. While the attraction of any organization may relate to a number of factors, including geographical location, perceived 'reputation' reflecting academic success and general standards of behaviour, is a considerable draw (Woods et al., 1998). Consequently, for many schools, it is not only a question of maintaining or increasing the number on roll, but for long-term sustainable recruitment, the 'right' kind of learners must be attracted. The profile of learners must be adjusted towards a profile which has the maximum number of students likely to achieve more than five A*–Cs at GCSE, or at least a reasonable percentage. In this way the position in the league table will be maintained or improved and the attraction of the school will not be diminished.

In parallel, post-16, school sixth forms and colleges must balance enrolling the largest number with excluding those who will not stay and achieve, or those who may involve too high additional costs (such as those with SLDD), resulting in a net expenditure loss rather than gain (Lumby, 1996). 'Successful' schools may well be in a powerful position to accept and reject learners as they think fit. Schools and colleges working in disadvantaged locations, or with disadvantaged communities are targeting those least likely to enrol, least likely to be retained and least likely to achieve accreditation either pre- or post-16. Such learners often involve additional costs, for example, to pay for access to vocational education provided externally, or for additional pastoral and learning support. Virtuous and vicious circles result, and the effect of these on schools and colleges and on the learning of 14–19-year-olds is the focus of the remainder of this chapter, where we trace through the effects at organizational level and at individual level upon the experience of learners.

Effects on schools and colleges

The funding context described has had an impact on the curriculum, on teaching and learning, on the profile of staff and on the focus and activity of leader/managers. The first three are explored in this chapter. The effect on leaders/managers is discussed in Chapter 11.

The principle of funding following the learner and learner achievement has led to a number of effects on the curriculum, experienced differentially throughout the system:

- Entry to courses/subjects may be restricted to those whose participation will not jeopardize the accreditation results which will determine success in accessing funding in the long term.
- Class sizes are increased.
- Courses/subjects which maximize income are increased.
- Courses/subjects or individuals which cost rather than generate income are minimized or excluded.
- Courses are reshaped to attract the maximum funding.

In summary, development of the curriculum has been skewed towards ensuring a profile which will attract and retain as many learners as possible in as lucrative ways as possible. In schools, the National Curriculum has to some degree protected core provision. However, even here learning may be influenced by resource issues. The development of vocational routes for 14–16-year-olds is one example. Vocational courses offered in partnership with local further education colleges have been constrained. First, the pressure to reach GCSE targets has led some schools to limit participation to those not likely to succeed in GCSEs. Additionally, the finite availability of additional Pathfinder project funds has rendered schools cautious in opening too widely a route which they may have to fund from their core budget in the future (Lumby and Morrison, 2004). Therefore, although a wider curriculum is in theory available to 14–19-year-olds, access is constrained by the problem which has surfaced in relation to many government pilot initiatives, concerns about long-term sustainable funding.

A further factor shaping development is the degree of competition. Schools for 14–16-year-olds may be happy for learners to become familiar with further education as an encouragement to stay on after 16. Schools with sixth forms may be more reluctant, wishing to retain within their own provision as many learners, and the consequent funding, as is feasible (Keys and Maychell, 1998; Schagen et al., 1996). In this way, the principle of funding following the learner, the competition induced by the quasi-market and the use of ring-fenced project funding to support development act in synergy to shape and constrain the development of the 14–16 curriculum.

Released from the bonds of the National Curriculum, post-16 provision has been more strongly influenced by funding. First, while organizations have always had to take account of the viability of particular courses, both the quantum of funding and the funding methodology have led many schools and colleges to shed more ruthlessly any which are likely to lose funds, to prioritize those which are likely to earn most and to increase class sizes to maximize income for each course. If funding follows the learner, then courses which are popular, irrespective of whether they are likely to lead to positive outcomes in terms of employment, will increase. Nursery-nursing and childcare saw a rapid 145 per cent growth in colleges after 1993, nearly double the growth of the next most popular, sciences, which grew by 79 per cent (Belfield et al., nd). The LEA may have previously co-ordinated provision so that unjustifiably large numbers of young people trained in any one vocational area were not produced. The funding liberated colleges from such restraint and, as Felstead and Unwin (2001) point out, the result was large cohorts of nursery-nurses and leisure and tourism graduates exiting at 19 to enter a labour market which did not necessarily need them.

Teaching and learning have been reshaped to attract funding. For example, provision which may have been seen previously as enrichment, and not necessarily accredited, now must conform to requirements to ensure accreditation and, therefore, funds. Key skills are one example within both schools and colleges where there is evidence of young people being, in effect, forced to undertake accredited programmes which they may view as unsuitable and unnecessary. In the words of one year 12 student, echoing the views of the majority in a study of sixth form colleges 'Key skills sucks, big time' (Lumby and Briggs, 2002, p. 54). Teachers, too, vary in their commitment. Independent schools generally do not bother with them at all. The real drive for providers is the funds they bring, rather than educational necessity. The DfEE has acknowledged the dubious effect of imposing study post-16:

> There is a gulf between the concept of Key Skills as espoused by policymakers and the lived reality of Key Skills as practised in classrooms and workplaces. Skilbeck et al (1994) raise interesting questions about the 'ownership' of these skills and raise doubts about their acceptability among people for whom they are presumed to be relevant yet whom were not consulted about their definition or development. (DfEE, 1999, para. 46)

Key skills is a good example of the use of funds to influence and the effects on teaching and learning. While not formally compulsory post-16, on the introduction of Curriculum 2000 the attachment of funds to key skills led many providers to insist that learners achieve such accreditation, a clear instance of funding leading to imposed study. In other areas, the effect of funding has been to shape the experience to match the 'guided learning hours' requirement, so that hours are increased or decreased to match particular funding requirements. Additionally, contact hours have decreased, more time being given to self-study often in newly constituted learning resource centres (Lumby, 1996; McDonald and Lucas, 2001).

There is some evidence that the availability of additional funds has enabled schools and colleges positively to encourage young people with special learning needs or disabilities to enrol, and has increased awareness and availability of support for students who may have a very wide range of learning needs (Lumby and Briggs, 2002). However, even exemplary organizations sometimes find the funding is not adequate to cover all the costs, but proceed anyway, driven by commitment to the individual learner.

Overall, in both schools and colleges, the effect of funding being dependent on student numbers has focused curriculum activity on maintaining a position where the level of recruitment will not be jeopardized. Output-related funding has, arguably, led to a positive focus on raising achievement, the intention, but has also led to a range of unintended effects, distorting the curriculum and shaping teaching towards maximizing accredited outcomes and, therefore, income rather than learning.

The staff profile

Schools and colleges control their own staffing budget. They cannot rely on an external body to fully fund agreed pay rises, or to deal with shortfalls in the budget to pay existing staff. The entrepreneurialism released by such independence has manifested itself in both positive inventiveness to access and fruitfully use resources, and in negative inappropriate commercial activity (Kennedy, 1997). Which is the case in any instance is, of course, a matter of judgement and will vary from person to person. The variety of opinion is nowhere more apparent than in responses to the way staffing has been adjusted in relation to financial pressures.

As discussed in Chapter 3, the number and nature of staff have been modified both in schools and colleges. The most dramatic effects have been experienced in further education colleges, where a large number of redundancies post-1993 were followed by the employment of much larger numbers of part-time, temporary and contract staff. Consequently, learners might expect to engage with a much wider range of people in the course of their learning experience, many of whom are not qualified teachers, but have specific roles such as instructor, assessor, learning adviser and so on. A parallel, if less pronounced, process is evident in schools. The expanded use of classroom assistants has been the subject of negotiation and disagreement between the government and teaching unions. While the government is promoting the use of assistants to release teaching staff from administrative and other non-essential duties, teachers fear that their role is being deprofessionalized and, for example, using classroom assistants to take a class as cover for an absent teacher is a clear case of using lesser paid and trained staff for teaching duties (Ward, 2003).

For many the use of 'paraprofessionals' to support teaching and learning is a direct result of inadequate funding, threatening the quality of teaching and learning by the use of unqualified staff. To others, the use of a wider range of staff not only offers legitimate savings, reserving expensive teachers for where they are essential, but also offers other advantages in bringing learners into contact with a greater variety of people who bring different experience and life views. Reflecting this view, the possibility of using non-qualified teachers in CTCs is an example of where the commercial or technical expertise of those outside the teaching profession has been promoted as a positive addition and not a detriment. No definitive judgement on these two positions is possible. What is clear is that the process of varying staff and looking carefully at the impact on costs has been accelerated by the twin factors of relative financial independence and financial pressure.

The effects on learning

What, then, has been the impact of funding on the experience of 14–19-year-olds? It is possible to distinguish direct and indirect effects. Direct effects are changes in the provision of learning opportunities or the practice of educators related to the amount of funding available or the method of its distribution. Indirect effects are those which result from changes to create or avoid a situation which will have a positive or negative impact on accessing income. Shutting down courses is a direct effect. Excluding troublesome pupils so the school's reputation will not suffer, thereby protecting the school from a possible drop in roll, is an indirect effect. Of course, funding may not be the only distinguishable cause of an effect. Sometimes the influence of funding may be enhanced or minimized by other factors.

Opportunities

From the start of secondary education, opportunities are shaped by the indirect influence of funding. Specifically, entry to particular schools has been shaped by changes in the sources of funding. City technology colleges and specialist schools access funds or resources from the community to offer facilities and an experience not available in the generality of comprehensives. Such 'specialness' has led to assumptions about who should have access. Walford (2000) describes the necessity for working-class families to show they are deserving of such opportunities. Families must be aware of the school and present a case for entry, convincing the school of the motivation, commitment and likelihood of success of their child. In this way the capital from industry invested in the school must be matched by the social capital of families: 'Those families who can show themselves to be "deserving" are far more likely to gain a place than others. Thus children from families with little interest in education are ignored' (Walford, 2000, pp. 154–5).

The previous selection for grammar schools by the ability of the individual has been replaced by selection of the family by social capital. The 'choice of school' at 11 is not primarily about the whole school experience but a choice based on what is available at 14 onwards, the GCSE years. The school's choice of entrants at 11 is equally more about the profile they will have at 14 and be able to retain (for 11–18 schools) at 16.

The 14–19 phase dominates the dance of choice, even though choice is undertaken at 11.

At 14 the ordering of options to be cost-effective and to maintain or increase attainment levels may influence the opportunities available. The vocational route may be open to few because of cost and because of a reluctance to jeopardize the schools' targets by allowing some young people to undertake vocational qualifications whose points value may be less than GCSEs (Lumby and Morrison, 2004).

At 16 young people may come under pressure, if they are in an 11–18 school, to remain in the school, unless they are not likely to be successful in achieving qualifications in which case they may come under pressure to leave (Keys and Maychell, 1998; Schagen et al., 1996). Risk-taking on the part of the school, in accepting those who may cost money by receiving teaching but not necessarily achieving their intended qualification, is discouraged by the funding methodology. Colleges within the Learning and Skills sector face the same dilemma.

The courses available may be more limited than those pre-1993. High-cost courses such as engineering have reduced, in part, because of their cost. Work-based learning, often undertaken by private training companies, dependent on output-related funding, will recruit carefully to those areas of training most likely to lead to jobs. Low-cost, low-duration training leading quickly to employment are more likely to be available to 16-year-olds (Felstead and Unwin, 2001). In schools, colleges and work-based learning there is little question of matching learning to specific learner needs where this falls outside what is perceived as cost-effective. Whole qualifications must be the target, as they attract funding, and the range of target qualifications must be cost-effective options. Rather than funding encouraging consideration of the individual learner, the effect has been often to narrow opportunities and to privilege those who have academic ability and/or social capital.

The experience of learning

The indirect effect of the funding system with a heavy emphasis on teaching to achieve successful accreditation outcomes was explored in Chapter 7. Funding constraints may have also contributed to a rise in class sizes. The average secondary school class has risen from 20.9 in 1993 to 21.9 in 2003 (DfES, 2004b). The average class size for year 10 in 2003 was 22.1 and for year 11, 21.4. The slight rise in average does not indicate the range of sizes. In 1993 4.7 per cent of secondary classes comprised over 30 learners. In 2003 the percentage of classes comprising 31 or more learners had risen to 8 per cent. Consequently, nearly one in ten secondary learners is taught in a class of over 30. For years 12 and 13 the hours available for each subject and for enrichment and pastoral support are likely to have reduced. Lumby and Briggs (2002) found that there was little difference in the pastoral time given to 16–19-year-olds in schools and general further education colleges. Sixth form colleges have retained a higher level of pastoral support, though they have not avoided the other effects of larger class sizes and shorter contact hours. Tables 9.1 and 9.2 show the range of hours in each type of institution.

Table 9.1 *Hours given per term to group tutorials in sixth form and general further education colleges and schools*

Group tutorials/term	SFC %	FE %	SCH %
0–5hrs	7.27	4.55	14.18
6–10hrs	10.91	18.18	20.90
11–15hrs	27.27	54.55	31.72
16–20hrs	36.36	4.55	17.16
21–25hrs	12.73	4.55	7.84
26+hrs	5.45	13.64	8.21
Mode	16–20 hrs	11–15 hrs	11–15 hrs
Median	16–20 hrs	11–15hrs	11–15 hrs

Source: Lumby and Briggs, 2002: 46

Table 9.2 *Hours given per term to individual tutorials in sixth form and general further education colleges and schools*

Individual tutorials/term	SFC %	FE %	SCH %
0–5hrs	42.59	72.73	76.14
6–10hrs	33.33	22.73	17.42
11–15hrs	11.11	0.00	3.79
Over 15hrs	12.96	4.55	2.65
Mode	0–5 hrs	0–5 hrs	0–5 hrs
Median	6–10 hrs	0–5 hrs	0–5 hrs

Source: Lumby and Briggs, 2002: 47

The multiple effects of larger class sizes, reduced contact hours and an imperative to achieve accreditation have driven much teaching back towards the didactic and shallow, rather than deep, learning (Harris et al., 1995; Lumby and Briggs, 2002).

Funding and 14–19 education

The primary aims of reform of the funding system for education have been to raise achievement and to widen participation. Fourteen to nineteen education is central in this strategy, crossing as it does the last moment of accreditation in the compulsory system and the point at which young people can exit. The national intentions in developing this period of education have been critical in shaping funding, and the reshaped system has in its turn had an impact upon the experience of 14–19 education. What, then, in summary, has been the impact of the way schools and colleges are resourced?

Raising achievement

The government points to a rise in the percentage of young people achieving five or more GCSEs at A*–C. The figures appear to indicate a clear trend towards improvement (Figure 9.1). Furthermore, the Prime Minister's website claimed that figures show that GCSE and GNVQ results in traditionally lower performing schools were improving over twice as quickly as other schools (10 Downing Street, 2004). Setting aside the almost annual debate on whether examinations are becoming easier and that this is the explanation for rising pass rates, numerous statisticians and educational commentators have challenged the use of statistics, and particularly the conclusions arrived at (Goldstein, 2001). Woods and Levačić (2002) argue that the schools which make the most progress are those which start from a low base. Consequently the claim that schools in challenging circumstances are improving faster than others is no surprise and not an indication, as implied, of the efficacy of government policy. Nevertheless, the approximate 10 per cent rise on those achieving five or more A*–C GCSEs from 1992 to 2002 is evidence of change, though repeating the argument developed in Chapter 7, it is evidence of a rise in accreditation, not learning. The two things cannot be assumed to be the same. The figures also might equally be seen as still leaving nearly half of young people missing what is seen by many as a minimum level of competence. Certainly the government has acknowledged the really serious problems for 14–19 education in the brief for the Tomlinson review.

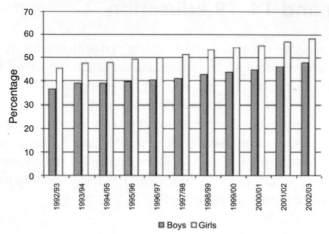

Figure 9.1
Percentage of pupils aged 15 achieving five or more GCSEs at grades A* to C, England, 1992/93 to 2002/03 (DfES, 2004a)

Reality check

Levačić and Glover (1998) suggest that only 11 per cent of the variance between the quality of learning between schools can be explained by resource deployment, and that the socio-economic context is more influential. Nevertheless, the indirect effects of the funding system may be profound in contributing to a culture which has shifted what learning means and how it is experienced by 14–19-year-olds. This chapter has argued that the direct and indirect effect of the level and distribution of resource has resulted in a curriculum focused on assessment, not learning, and on maximizing income, and has impelled organizations to put their own best interests at least as high as that of individual learners (Foskett et al., 2004). The results of this change in culture may be even more insidious. The culture change brought about in part by the funding system, attested repeatedly in the literature (Gleeson, 2001; Kennedy, 1997; Simkins, 2000) where those that cannot offer 'value' to schools and colleges in hard cash terms may feel themselves of less value as people, cannot be ignored as a factor in the shaping of society, the perspective of young people and their sense of worth. The way in which the national investment in 14–19 educations is shaped may elicit a direct response from young people who respond with investment of their own, but not necessarily in education, and not necessarily in the schools and colleges where the system, impelled strongly by finance, implies their uncertain worth.

Chapter 10

Working together? Collaboration and partnerships for learning

Perhaps the most significant difference between the education and training sector in the twenty-first century and that of the 1970s has been the dismantling of the command and control system encapsulated in the government–LEA–school/college hierarchy, and its replacement with the twin-axis model of strong central government direction and autonomous individual institutions. Between the two sits a wide range of professional, commercial and/or bureaucratic organizations that operate in an environment of markets, choice, and partnership, such as LEAs, LLSCs, Connexions organizations, training companies and educational consultancies. Government strategy for the management of education and training has been to 'draw a wider range of agencies into the process of educational improvement. National policy is intended to be enabling and creative rather than directive and constraining. Partnerships have replaced formal accountability hierarchies in the rhetoric of government ministers and officials' (Bennett et al., 2004, p. 218).

The twin pressures of competition and an emphasis on the importance of partnerships in supporting learning 14–19 have pushed schools and colleges to examine how they work with this wide range of 'external' organizations. As young people move from Key Stage 3 into the 14–19 phase they cross a significant boundary. In Key Stages 1–3 education is focused almost entirely within the school and its own resources, but from the start of Key Stage 4 the expertise of a wide range of stakeholders outside the school begins to play a major part. Provision by colleges, by vocational training organizations and by local employers appears within the potential learning diet of young people in school. As a consequence a vision for an integrated 14–19 phase is *de facto* a vision of strong partnership and collaboration. As the DfES has suggested:

It would not be possible for every individual school, college or work-

place to deliver every aspect of the 14–19 curriculum. Therefore we
expect them to work together to provide students with their 14–16
entitlement, to provide more choice and to make it easier for young
people to move from pre- to post-16 learning.

... In particular, consistent partnerships between learning and
business need to develop quickly. Strong links between schools, colleges and employers are vital to support the greater emphasis on
work-related and enterprise learning. (DfES, 2003h, p. 6)

A central tenet of government policy, therefore, is organizational partnership and collaboration or OPC (Glatter, 2003). In its summary of
proposals, *14–19: Opportunity and Excellence* (DfES, 2003h), this commitment is underlined by the DfES: 'Our vision for the 14–19 phase is one
where ... schools and colleges are working in partnership and innova-
tively to meet the needs of all learners' (DfES, 2003h, p. 3). Similarly, for
schools the DfES (2003f) has identified collaboration with external
organizations as one of the six core principles for school improvement.
This chapter examines the nature of these partnerships, and considers
the strategic and management implications of developing these relationships in an effective and efficient way.

Why partnership?

The commitment to partnership is rooted in a number of environmental
forces that have characterized both the 14–19 sector and education and
training in general since the realignment of the public sector with the
core values of accountability that emerged in the post-Ruskin speech era.

The first key driver is the political dimension of accountability itself.
Prior to 1979 the simple chain of relationships connected the government to LEAs to schools and colleges in a linear form. Since 1979, by
seeking to 'wrest power from the professional' (O'Hear, 1991, p. 17) the
government has engaged a wide range of bodies external to schools and
colleges in the provision of education services and in the judgement of
their effectiveness. The relationships between this diverse range of players on the education and training stage, ranging from schools to colleges,
to funding bodies (for example, FEFC/LSC), to inspection organizations
(for example, OFSTED), to service providers, to employers, are manifold
and variable, not least in terms of the balance of power between them.

But underlying this ecological web of relationships is the view that the interests of the learner and, particularly, of the government lie best where no single organization holds dominant control and where many parts of society contribute to shaping the nature and organization of the education and training business. Each player is regarded as a stakeholder, each is charged with a specific role or niche within the web, each is expected to contribute synergistically what they are best equipped to provide to the education and training service, and each provides checks and balances to the function and quality of the others. More importantly, though, by limiting the power and authority in any single part of the system the government very effectively retains power in its own hands. The rhetoric of accountability to the market and to the learner is in reality the retention and enhancement of accountability to the government.

It is perhaps ironic that a key component of the accountability engendered in partnership is that of 'trust', which is in itself intimately linked to notions of professionalism – the very perspective that was a target of educational reform in the 1980s and 1990s. Mordaunt (1999), Glatter (2003) and Bennett et al. (2004) all stress the importance of trust as a critical factor in the success of partnerships. Bottery (2002), in a discussion of the nature of trust, has emphasized how 'role trust', which is recognized in a relationship by assumptions according to an individual's professional role and the implicit knowledge of an occupation's set of ethics, is important in facilitating rapid development of trust-based relationships. We explore later how critical such trust is to the effective operation of partnership.

The second key driver is financial, although as with accountability there is a reality that contradicts the rhetoric. As discussed in Chapter 9, the expansion of the education system post-16 particularly and the pursuit of higher education, training and skill levels requires financial investment, yet the downward pressures on public finance have encouraged governments to adopt the values and processes of markets to promote the achievement of value for money and economic efficiency. The rhetoric is that the accountabilities of the education web will themselves act as an effective audit process, and promote the financial economies that come from specialization and competition. Perhaps more importantly, the presence of strong government financial control requires schools and colleges to develop managed external relationships to optimize the resources they can access. The reality is that the economies of such an approach are hard to identify. The establishment and maintenance of partnership is highly demanding of time, management energy and direct costs.

The epistemological driver is the third force towards external partnership. This has two components, one associated with the skills and knowledge of educational organizations, and one associated with the learners themselves. The strong shift away from the teacher as the only knowledge authority towards learning based on student needs and individualized learning places a demand for a wide range of sources and forms of knowledge to be accessible to learners. For the learner to access this diversity of knowledge, the organization itself must draw on a wide range of evidence and knowledge to enhance its own practices and systems. Griffiths (2000, pp. 384–5) argues that 'collaboration leads to better knowledge ... (and) for collaboration to be successful it is crucial that diverse perspectives are incorporated into the outcomes of an initiative'. In this way, both the knowledge that the students themselves can access and the knowledge of the most effective ways of facilitating that access are enhanced by the processes of collaboration. So, even without accountability and financial drivers there is a strong educational pressure for partnership.

The fourth driver towards partnership is an operational one. One of the consequences of marketization and self-management that has characterized the 1990s in particular has been the emergence of what Glatter (2003, p. 17) terms 'organisational fragmentation' in the context of an increasingly complex and diverse education and training service. Storey (1998) has suggested that as the operating environments of organizations change, so organizational structures and forms must change too. In a command system the dominant form of organization is bureaucracy, while as the environment changes towards that of the market so the focus on performance by organizations will drive them towards different ways of operating. As Edem et al. (2003, p. 39) suggest:

> (Storey's model) suggests that the shift towards greater involvement with outsourcing, joint ventures and networks is related to the move towards diversification, performance-based control and more open markets. It is possible to see such shifts in the post-16 learning sector, with the increasing demands of a performance-based responsibility ... (This) is leading organisations to become more externally-focused.

Networks and partnerships are promoted, therefore, as providing higher quality and more flexible provision with the focus of activity on the needs of the individual learner. This may happen in a voluntaristic way in response to general environmental changes, but is also happening in response to statutory obligation. From 2004, schools teaching young people in Key Stage 4 have a statutory obligation to provide work-related learning for all students, to enable them to learn through experience of work, learn about work and working practices, and learn skills for work. This requirement means that schools will need to enhance their collaboration with employers and business in their locality to support the work-related learning, which may act as a stimulus to the development of wider partnerships.

This has generated a concern both for coherence across the system and equity in the service and opportunity for young learners. Just as individual teachers are no longer the sole arbiters of knowledge, so the school or college cannot be the sole source of expertise for every function and service that the school and learners require. Schools, for example, cannot realistically have teaching staff to provide expertise in a full range of vocational fields, but can access those skills and services from places where they can be provided economically. Enabling school students to access vocational courses at the local FE college, buying in consultancy services or payroll services, or accessing IAG expertise through the Connexions service, all illustrate the value and sense of collaboration and partnership in such a fragmented system. Furthermore, a response to fragmentation has arisen from the context of the professional nature of those working in education, in that there has been a strong call for development of networks of mutual support and engagement within education and training. Such horizontal relationships provide a valued replacement for the declining vertical control systems of, for example, LEAs (Hargreaves, 2003).

The nature of partnership

The relationship between organizations in education and training fall essentially into three types – control, autonomy and partnership. Within the 14–19 sector all three forms of relationship exist, although their relative importance has changed substantially in the last two decades.

Control is exercised, for example, through the financial allocation models for post-16 learning of local Learning and Skills Councils, and by the statutory control of the Key Stage 4 curriculum by the government. Autonomy exists in the freedom of institutions to choose their own market profile and appoint their own staff. These two forms of relationship are the most prominent within the system today. So what is the nature of the third type of relationship, partnership?

We have presented the notion of partnership so far as if it is an unproblematic concept based on ideas such as 'working together', 'common aims', 'mutual benefit' and 'equity', and also as if in the light of the pressures towards partnership outlined above that it is universally regarded as 'a good thing'. Neither of these perspectives is true, however, and for most organizations and individuals working in the 14–19 sector partnership is problematic and challenging.

Some of the concerns about partnership can be identified in the history of the development of the concept. Prior to 1979 relationships between schools and colleges were usually superficially collaborative but operationally detached. The strength of shared professional values meant that a rhetoric of engagement and dialogue existed, and in some cases, where LEAs acted as strong brokers, supported a genuinely collaborative culture. More frequently, however, the connections between schools and colleges, and between colleges, LEAs and employers, were at least semi-detached and frequently almost totally detached. Post-1979, and more strongly post-1988, any culture of partnership was strongly compromised by marketization, competition and central accountability and control. Although organizations were still expected to manage relations with a range of stakeholders from parents to industrial organizations, the dominant relationships were competitive, transactional or accountability based. Competitive relationships were those with other education and training providers, where each organization sought to establish a strong position in the local education/training marketplace. Transactional relationships were those based on supplier–purchaser processes. Accountability-based relationships were those with inspection bodies and those organizations providing funding for the education and training service, including TECs and LEAs.

After 1997, however, the balance between these types of external relationships began to shift, and partnership became a more highly vaunted concept. In schools, while the government continued to emphasize their autonomy and accountability, the importance of partnership in ensuring the raising of pupil achievement emerged strongly through the 1997 White Paper *Excellence in Schools* (DfEE, 1997c). Similarly in the FE sector a shift from competitive cultures began to be seen as critical to progress towards government targets on widening participation and raising achievement. Kennedy (1997), in her seminal report *Learning Works*, suggested that competition rather than partnership had impeded progress towards widening participation, and promoted the idea of strong partnerships involving all local stakeholders as an essential step towards redressing the problems. However, following a period in which partnerships had frequently died or been compromised, the will, knowledge and expertise to create and maintain effective partnerships was too frequently found to be absent.

So what range of relationships can we identify within the 14–19 arena? It has been usual to classify external relationship either in terms of their function/purpose or in terms of the nature of the relationship between the parties. Hence Foskett (1999) offers a functional classification that distinguishes between transactional-based, relationship-based and public accountability based external relations in schools and colleges. Hall (1999), in focusing on the nature of the relationship itself, supports Glatter (1996) in considering that the traditional dichotomy between collaborative and competitive relationships is too simplistic, and suggests a continuum of ways of working between either individuals or organizations. She suggests that this continuum ranges from relationships based on conflict, which are negative and founded in the pursuit of win–lose outcomes, to relationships based on collaboration, which are positive in character and based on the pursuit of win–win outcomes. Between these extremes lie competitive relationships (principally negative and based on win–lose), co-ordination relationships (neutral in both dimensions) and co-operative relationships that are essentially positive and based on win–win perspectives.

Partnerships are characterized, therefore, by the pursuit of mutual benefits, to achieve a win–win situation. However, they are not uniquely like this, for any specific partnership may have elements of different relationships within it. For example, post-16 colleges may form a partnership to collaborate to promote progression from Key Stage 4 to post-16 study. In minority curriculum areas they may even agree to focus provision in one or other institution (for example, Music A level in college A only, Spanish A level in college B only). Across most of the curriculum, though, they will still be in a competitive arena, with each college seeking to maximize recruitment to their own English AS or AVCE Leisure and Tourism programmes.

Partnerships may also be variable in their formality. Indeed, the growth of professional networks and learning networks (Hargreaves, 2003) has involved the evolution of a form of partnership which is largely informal, and contrasts quite strongly with the formality of partnerships such as Education Action Zones or 14–19 Pathfinder Partnerships. Although a prominent form of relationship, it has been argued by Lowndes and Skelcher (1998) that networks, therefore, are different in concept than 'partnerships' because of their emphasis on voluntary association between organizations rather than on a formal, explicitly managed and planned activity.

Managing partnerships

All educational organizations contend within their strategic plans, their mission statements and their management rhetoric that partnership and collaboration are a central part of their way of working within the 14–19 sector. Managing partnerships within 14–19 requires an initial understanding of some of the features of partnership working. Research into the nature of partnerships in education has not yet been extensive, and relates mainly to the evaluation of particular OPC initiatives. As a phenomenon mainly of the 1990s, there have been comparatively few studies which have sought to evaluate partnerships, not least because it is generally recognized that partnerships must evolve over a period of time and do not necessarily support quick wins. Glatter (2003), for example, draws on some of the evidence from within and outside education that demonstrates the organizational and managerial challenges and problems of achieving the outcomes that partnerships set. The overall picture is one of under-achievement and challenge, because 'partnership processes can be slow and painful and ... partnerships often do not deliver what was expected of them. Although this may seem discouraging, it can also be reassuring in indicating that particular problems are common and not just the result of individuals' incompetence or poor practice' (Glatter, 2003, pp. 18–19).

The reasons for such underachievement are complex, and vary of course from partnership to partnership. However, drawing on the work of McQuaid (2000) and Huxham and Vangen (2000), Glatter suggests that there are seven common problems that handicap the success of partnerships:

- unclear goals, such that the whole partnership or individual partners are not sure of what the goals are
- resource costs, both in terms of the cost of the project activity and the cost of sustaining the partnership
- unequal power, where this is not recognized as a key characteristic of the partnership
- cliques usurping power
- impacts upon other mainstream services, so that the work on the partnership detracts from or contradicts other activities
- differences in philosophy between partners
- organizational problems in managing or operationalizing the partnership activities.

From this summary of the reasons for failure we can begin to identify the critical success factors for partnership. Both Mordaunt (1999) and Glatter (2003) have sought to clarify these critical factors, and from their perspectives we can derive a useful checklist:

1. The objectives of the partnership must be clear and explicit.
2. There must be a focus on a single issue or a narrow range of outcomes.
3. There must be common values around goodwill, trust and agreed operating procedures.
4. It must be recognized that all partners are driven by self-interest.
5. Each partner must derive benefits from the partnership.
6. The partnership must be for 'the greater good' and not simply for the benefit of partners.
7. Partners must be free to exit from the partnership if they choose.
8. It must be recognized that all partners are not necessarily equal. This may relate to the size and contribution of the organization to the inputs of the partnership or to the relative benefits that derive from it, and may even relate to the power relations within the partnership (McQuaid, 2000).
9. Each partner will bring a distinctive contribution to the partnership.

10. Each partner has its own identity, culture and history.
11. Partnership involves trade-offs, compromises and flexibility.
12. Partners need to nurture the partnership continuously.
13. There must be clear, predetermined lines of communication and decision-making.
14. The relationship will be dynamic and will evolve over time.

The length of this list underlines the complexity and challenge of managing successful partnership, and provides a useful benchmark against which to examine real examples of partnership in action.

Bennett et al. (2004) have examined the nature of the partnership between schools and LEAs from the perspective of six chief education officers (CEOs). The change in the relationship, from one of LEA control to one of partnership, is expressed clearly by the LEAs, as the autonomy of the schools means that they must choose the precise nature of the relationship they have with their LEAs. Despite this autonomy, though, Bennett et al. (2004, p. 233) conclude that 'the characteristics of a successful partnership are absent' and that 'the conditions for true partnership may be inhibited by both the schools and the external national environment'. Specifically, Bennett et al. suggest that in the case of the six LEAs a number of key elements of partnership were largely missing. Schools and the LEAs were largely unwilling to surrender any degree of individual autonomy, and there was little mutual accountability in the pursuit of shared goals and shared decision-making. Partnerships were not seen to be voluntary associations, with schools engaging with the LEAs because of the statutory obligation upon them to collaborate on specified issues such as funding rather than because of a genuine belief in the value of the partnership. Finally, partners did not perceive themselves as equal but different, but both groups of partners regarded themselves as the key power within the relationship.

These observations show that many of the critical factors for partnership identified in our earlier checklist were not being met. As a result the schools and LEA had made little progress on developing explicit, mutually agreed goals, and Bennett et al. (2004, p. 228) conclude that: 'In the view of the CEOs, many schools had not yet achieved the maturity that would make it possible for all parties to acknowledge the different accountabilities of each.'

While acknowledging that the research represents the perspectives of the CEOs and LEAs for whom the shift to partnership involves a substantial change in their previously dominant power position, there seems to be some evidence that the development of partnerships is evolutionary and requires significant changes of attitudes and approaches from all partners. The potential for benefit from partnership is significant although:

> [I]n the eyes of the CEOs, the schools and the LEAs could achieve more if they worked together (but) this clear expectation of 'collaborative advantage' (Huxham and Vangan, 2000) is largely absent from the view of ... school-based interviewees ... for whom the LEA role was one of subservient support, to be called upon as required and defined by the individual school. (Bennett et al., 2004, pp. 230–1)

The pattern of high potential and, as yet, limited progress towards effective partnership is reported in other research, too. Edem et al. (2003) provide a picture of the national patterns of partnership in post-16 education and training. They conclude that while there are many excellent examples of partnership, the pattern is patchy, and there is 'a marked absence, in general, of clear overall area-wide and city-wide strategies' (Edem et al., 2003, p. 25) for partnership. In almost every arena of partnership they are able to identify examples of good practice, for example, in relation to:

- collaboration between schools and colleges in a locality through, for example, common timetabling of AS/A2 courses as between the schools and FE college in Abingdon
- collaboration between colleges, for example in the North-East Colleges Network which provides networked, flexible on-line training across 15 FE colleges
- learning partnerships, for example with the Liverpool Lifelong Learning Partnership which has drawn key partners together in the city
- engagement of schools and colleges with work-based learning providers, as exemplified in Bradford in the connection between Bradford College, local schools, the local LSC and local employers who have formed the West Yorkshire Learning Providers Network
- education–business links, for example, the Bridge Project in the Craven area of North Yorkshire, providing training and work experi-

ence for year 10 pupils
- the establishment of federal post-16 learning structures, as for example in Sheffield and in Greenwich
- work with the careers or Connexions service.

However, Edem et al. (op. cit) emphasize the enormous variation in patterns and effectiveness of partnership. They attribute this to a number of key factors within local operational environments. First, the patterns of school and college provision are important in this, for whether a locality is organized with 11–18 schools, 11–16 schools, sixth form colleges or FE colleges drives the fundamental competitive or collaborative context. Foskett et al. (2004) have demonstrated how a competitive environment between 11–18 schools and FE/sixth form colleges militates against partnership, while 11–16 schools often work very effectively with local post-16 providers. Secondly, the leadership and vision shown by the key local lead organizations, the LEAs and the LLSCs, can constrain or promote partnership. Thirdly, where there is a local history of partnership in 14–19, perhaps originating from TVEI consortia in the 1980s, there is often a more positive view of working together. Fourthly, the geographical characteristics of the 'travel to learn' region may act as a barrier to or enhancer of partnership. Foskett and Hesketh (1997), for example, distinguish between contiguous markets, where providers compete in a geographical locality, and parallel markets, where they do not. Fifth, and certainly of considerable importance, is the history of relationships between the partners and the presence or absence of trust. Partnerships are effectively between individuals rather than organizations, and a history of difficult relationships may handicap progress. In the 14–19 sector this may be a particular issue, for the phase of strong competitive markets of the early 1990s damaged many previously good and positive local relationships, which may, perhaps, only be repaired when new leaders arrive in organizations. Finally, an important factor is the influence of a key trigger to action that is seen unequivocally as a high priority. A common example is the recognition of low or declining post-16 participation rates, or the impact of OFSTED inspection commenting negatively on provision, either of which can lead to review of post-16 provision and the enhancement of collaboration. Edem et al. (op. cit) provide examples of such developments in Greenwich in south London and in Hammersmith, and evidence from evaluations of 14–19 Pathfinder projects suggests that the input of funding they provide acts as a catalyst for the development of relationships that would otherwise have been difficult (for example, Lumby and Morrison, 2004).

It is clear from this analysis that the establishment of effective partnership is potentially challenging and complex, with many component factors that can individually or in combination make or break potential partnership. In considering these issues the place of young people should be, of course, central to concerns – so what does this all mean for the learner? The move away from control-based models of organization to models based on institutional autonomy and partnership is, in part, predicated on the belief that this enhances the flexibility and responsiveness of the 14–19 system, and so enables a focus on the needs of the individual learner. Our earlier chapters have demonstrated the growth of increasingly individualized learning. What is in effect emerging is the notion of partnership between the learner and the school or college, based around providing for their individual learning needs and obliging the school, college or training organization to develop further partnerships to enable that to be delivered. But what impact does this have on the learner? It clearly brings him or her into contact with a wider range of learning experiences and a wider range of learning providers, the diversity and expertise of whom should provide improved learning. At the same time, though, that diversity and variety adds complexity. The simple model of teacher–learner that has traditionally characterized education, and training has always had the advantage of being a model that is simple to understand and within which it is simple to identify responsibility and accountability. It also enables the learner to travel through the system in a passive way, simply receiving the education and training they were given. The notion of partnership gives the learner both greater choice/benefit and a greater responsibility for proactive engagement with learning. The learner has to engage actively with the partnership or else, just as we have seen above in the case of school/LEA collaboration, the partnership will fall short of achieving its aims. The evolution of partnership models of operation applies, therefore, from institutions to individuals and from system-level to student-level.

Reality check

The rhetoric of partnership is an important element of the 14–19 education and training arena. Partnership has the potential to bring both individual benefits to organizations and to contribute to Mordaunt's idea of 'the greater good' if managed effectively. We have identified earlier, though, that there is only limited evidence of the establishment of partnership as the principle way of working in the 14–19 sector, and that the scene is characterized, rather, by contradiction, conflict and confusion.

Partnership has been encouraged as the new *modus operandi* in schools and colleges, but in reality it represents a thin curtain set to hide the continuance of existing practices and existing relationships. Partnership, indeed, may be ritualistic, with partners gaining individual kudos by the public presentation of a partnership that actually allows each of the partners to continue much as they have done in the past. Such partnerships of convenience or partnerships of ritual may lead to little real change, and in evaluating the effectiveness of any collaborative activity it may be important to question how far the relationship is real or chimera.

This idea of ritual is important to recognize. A relative lack of experience in partnership, and the strong underpinning demands of competitive relationships in the 14–19 marketplace, may make partnership unattractive to many organizations. Indeed, there are dangers in partnership for where the key features of partnership, the implicit rules of the game, are not adhered to we may recognize a relationship that is a partnership in name but is a competitive win–lose relationship in practice. Mordaunt (1999) terms such relationships 'predatory partnerships', and it is fear of the risks of such relationships that may be slowing progress. Our perspective is that progress towards partnership is occurring but that the tethers holding institutions to the self-centred demands of competition are still very strong and constraining. We conclude with the views of a sixth form college principal, whose perspective 'from the chalk face' confirms this view:

> The rhetoric of collaboration ... is still being held back in its progress to practice by the equally powerful machinery of competition. Much of what colleges do is still determined by the twin levers of funding and inspection, and these are embedded in a culture of competitiveness ... If we really want people and establishments to work together for the greater good, we have to find a new way to assess the effects when they do work together. (Thomson, 2004, p. 17)

Chapter 11

Leading 14–19 education: lifting our heads

Evidence?

Much of the discussion in the book so far directs us to considering leadership as a crucial element in improving 14–19 education. Developing teaching and learning, structure and partnership are dependent on the leadership of those with an organizational, local or regional responsibility. There is a large body of literature on leadership which should in theory offer insights into how leading 14–19 education might develop to build on successes and to overcome the difficulties and failures outlined in previous chapters. There are however some problems. First, the literature is divided into that which deals with schools and that which deals with colleges and work-based learning. With a few exceptions, the impression given reading this body of literature is that those researching schools are unaware of and uninterested in the education of 16–19-year-olds in colleges, and vice versa. There are also gaps. While the body of literature on schools is large, that on colleges is much smaller and largely concerned with general further education colleges. Leadership in sixth form colleges and work-based learning are not much reported. Consequently, the issue of leading 14–19 education is seen in fragmented form as leadership of all those in the age range who happen to stay on in school, a minority, or alternatively leadership of a portion of the age group, 16–18-year-olds. This chapter reviews what we know of leadership in each context and then explores how we might understand the challenge of leadership in a holistic sense for 14–19-year-olds.

Leadership enacted how?

The term 'leadership' has so far been used unproblematically, but defining its meaning remains a challenge. 'Commentators cannot agree upon a set of behaviour that amounts to leadership' (Gronn, 2000, p. 6). In other words we cannot say what leadership is with any clarity. This uncertainty has never stopped researchers and trainers from outlining the latest theory and suggested approach. One constant, however, has been the assumption that the effect of leadership on learning is the central concern. Hallinger and Heck (1996) point out that research has little to say convincingly on the link between leadership and learning, and that the literature is very partial and habitually focused on leadership of the principal rather than all those who might be understood to be engaged in leadership. In response, emphasis has increasingly been placed on distributed leadership (Harris, 2004; Lumby, 2003a), a vaguely conceived concept which 'concentrates on engaging expertise wherever it exists within the organisation rather than seeking this only through formal position or role' (Harris, 2004, p. 13). The jury is still out on whether this is simply rebadging delegated or collegial styles of leadership, or is a truly new way of approaching leadership. Certainly the idea of leadership as flowing from many, rather than few, resonates strongly with how 14–19 education is developing, with those supporting learning increasingly placed throughout a wider community.

Harris (2004, p. 14) suggests that distributed leadership implies that: 'The job of those in formal leadership positions is primarily to hold the pieces of the organization together in a productive relationship.' This inward-looking definition is too narrow for 14–19 education. The job of leaders of this age group is clearly to hold the pieces together not just in the organization, but much more widely, across organizations, and conceivably across the part-time work of many learners. Learning-centred leadership has been implicitly viewed as learning within one organization in a defined time span. For 14–19-year-olds, truly learning-centred leadership will focus on learning in a variety of settings and on a lifetime's time span. Leadership for 14–19-year-olds cannot equate to leading a school or a college.

Training leaders

This message is not evident in the preparation for leadership. The training for leaders of schools and leaders in the Learning and Skills Sector (LSS) studiously maintains a dividing gulf between the sectors and focuses inwards to the organization. The National College for School Leadership (NCSL) and the Centre for Excellence (offering leadership development for LSS staff) each focus on staff in one sector. Their funding demands results within that one sector, so cross-sectoral work is structurally impeded. There is then little chance for bridging the divide between leaders and leadership in the schools and LSS through their training. Additionally, the implied model of leadership embedded in their training is essentially concerned with improving achievement as assessed at organizational level. Leaders are trained to run effective schools and effective colleges or workplace learning, assessed most importantly by improvement in learners' test or examination outcomes. The LSS offers a business-based leadership model and the NCSL a public sector outputs-based model. As such their vision is equally sterile for 14–19 year olds, inward and backward looking. If 14–19-year-olds are to get a better deal, then it is the leaders themselves who must create a vision which is wider than the organization and more long term than what happens while learners are with them.

The purpose of leadership

While the narrowness of the earlier focus on the leadership of the principal has been challenged by the idea of distributed leadership, the narrowness of the focus on the *purpose* of leadership has not. Staff in schools often seem to place a low priority on addressing education *outcomes*, that is, young people entering employment, training or further education, or at least to place it much lower than targets concerned with education *outputs*, that is, examination and value-added scores. Though school leaders are assumed to genuinely favour the use of education to support a more egalitarian and socially just society, both external and internal factors may exert pressure in another direction. Schooling's long-standing uneasy relationship with both social reproduction and social justice has moved more into the spotlight with growing emphasis on 'the increasingly sophisticated analyses of social *in*justice as played out in schools' (Furman and Shields, 2003, p. 2). This raises the question, if leadership is for learning, then what is learning for? There is a growing sense that simply raising achievement may be insufficient, and that leadership must focus on outcomes, not just outputs. Put differently, there is a growing emphasis on leadership for social justice, and it is this imperative which is in part impelling reform of 14–19 education and training. However, just as broad aims about achieving potential and supporting learning can be used as mythology to conceal realities, commitment to social justice can serve a similar purpose. Educators have continued a rhetoric of equity through decades of inequitable actions and outcomes.

Furman and Shields (2003) argue that there are two contrary directions in understanding social justice. On the one hand, we have ever more specified lists of those whose particular needs must be met; the disabled, minority ethnic groups, children of gay families and so on. In contradiction to this concept of social justice which focuses on differentiating need is a different impetus, the attempt to be equitable or fair to all. Furman and Shields (2003) argue that being fair, that is, treating all the same, potentially works against social justice as this ignores different levels of need. Above all, they argue that leadership for social justice is about challenging differential power amongst the groups which shape education. As a result, in their view, 'leadership grounded in the moral purposes of democratic and community and social justice in schools is, first and foremost about pedagogy' (Furman and Shields, 2003, pp. 23–4). It follows that the primary task of leaders of 14–19 education is to find a socially just pedagogy.

There results a range of challenges for the leadership of 14–19 education:

- How can leaders look up and beyond their own organization to see leadership as providing opportunities for learning within the wider community?
- If leadership is for learning, what is learning for? Is learning the proper primary focus of leadership 14–19? If this is the case, in what sense should learning be understood as relevant to the whole range of learners and what is its relationship to life chances?

Approaches to leadership

School leadership

Leaders of 14–19 school education generally also lead 11–13 education within the same school, and the influence of younger children on the culture and style of leadership is profound. The legislative duty of care places leaders in *loco parentis* and thereby creates the same power differential and tensions between young people and school leaders as is the case between young people and their parents. The growing desire of young people for greater autonomy and for more adult relationships grows alongside a culture which is shaped by the needs of younger children as much as by those in the 14–19 age range. The resulting culture is one which many young people find inimical (Lumby and Morrison, 2004). Leaders face the difficulty of achieving a culture more suited to 14–19 learners. This is the first characteristic of school leadership which impacts on developing 14–19 education.

Secondly, leaders of schools, whether headteachers, deputies, middle leaders or teacher leaders, generally relate to a small enough group of staff to be personally aware of all staff and to have a personal relationship with most, if not all. Bush and Glover (2003, p. 3) suggest that distributed leadership 'takes place within a pattern of interpersonal relationships' rather than individual action. It would seem, then, that schools are better placed than are the much larger and often more dispersed FE colleges to use relationships as the basis for leadership. The relatively tightly knit community of the school is the foundation of the emphasis in the substantial literature on school leadership on cohesion, on building a vision to which all commit. The major role of the headteacher is frequently asserted to be building such vision and commitment. For example, Bush and Glover quote Begley who identifies four levels of vision-making, the most advanced of which is 'expert' whereby the headteacher 'collaborates with representative members of the school community to develop goals which reflect a collaboratively developed vision statement' (Bush and Glover, 2003, p. 5). The assumption within this statement is fairly typical in that it is inward looking towards the school. The vision is not created by a wider community of partners or even with this perspective in mind. Effective school leaders, particularly headteachers, run effective schools.

This dominant notion of school leadership is no longer adequate for 14–19 education. It is organization based, influenced by the needs of younger children and often focused on 'high standards' or 'raising achievement'. It is intimately connected to the credentialism which sees a rise in the percentage gaining A*–C GCSEs as the primary indicator of an improving school and effective leadership. In a study of schools and colleges in a 14–19 partnership, one deputy reflected on how each school was pursuing its own vision in its own way and questioned, 'If we are all in on this, why do we need different systems?' (Lumby and Morrison, 2004, p. 34). The intense focus on the single organization, the school, no doubt can work well for those learners whose pathway is exclusively within the school from 14 to 19, but for the majority who at 14 or at 16 will diverge and spend part or all of their time in another organization, the school vision is not likely to be adequate.

There are also practical factors, such as the conditions in school which will impel or impede leaders' development of 14–19 education. A national review of the state of school leadership (Earley et al., 2002) found that leaders are demotivated by excessive bureaucracy and constant change. The mix in school leadership of demotivation and inward lookingness does not bode well for developing 14–19 education.

Leadership in the Learning and Skills Sector

While leadership of secondary schools is not homogeneous, the range of approaches to leadership in the Learning and Skills Sector is much wider. The principal of a sixth form college may see his or her role as very similar to a secondary school principal. The leadership of a small company offering work-based training may have much more in common with the commercial approach of other small to medium-sized enterprises. Great care is therefore needed in exploring leadership in the LSS to differentiate between the various contexts (Lumby, 2003a).

Thrupp (1998) argues that leadership is to some degree shaped by the nature of the student profile, that leadership of a school of disadvantaged learners cannot be the same as that in a school with an advantaged population. Lumby (2003a) goes further and suggests that a number of factors have shaped leadership in the Learning and Skills Sector:

- student profile
- the competitive environment
- the stability/instability of the institution
- size
- the cohesiveness of the curriculum.

All of these factors, which vary much more than within secondary schools, result in a range of leadership approaches within the sector.

The *student profile* varies considerably from organization to organization. High-achieving sixth form colleges may appeal to and attract academic high flyers. By contrast, general further education colleges attract more students with lower academic prior attainment. The reasons for this are complex, but may be in part because general further education colleges (GFECs) offer an environment where the values and experience of both staff and student may be in tune with those of learners in the bottom quartile of academic achievement. It may be, therefore, that leadership of learning for disaffected 14–19-year-olds has a head start in colleges, in that the environment for learning is in key with the values, experience and aims of many of this group of learners.

Competition with schools, with other colleges, with training providers, with employment opportunities is acute. A survey in 2002 found that more than a third of colleges felt they were in competition with 10 or more schools, some with as many as 30. Seventy per cent of GFECs felt that the funding method exerted pressure to compete compared to only 45 per cent of schools (Lumby and Briggs, 2002). The intense competition results in a central imperative to recruit, retain and achieve, which is different in nature to school leaders dealing with a more captive audience.

The resource levels are therefore highly volatile, resulting in *instability*, and parts of the curriculum, staff and buildings may come and go relatively quickly. Organizational restructuring is a frequent event, as is restructuring of the local and regional administration of the sector. Leadership must relate to a turbulent environment, and issues of finance and survival figure strongly.

The size of organization in the sector varies considerably, with some small work-based training providers running with less than 10 staff while a large college may have over a 1,000 staff and service around 20,000 students. The distribution over several sites may also present the leadership with particular challenges. While schools may have split sites, the scale of number of staff/students and number of sites is sometimes considerably greater in the LSS and presents leaders with issues not experienced in the same way in schools.

Finally, leading what may be a *highly diverse curriculum*, academic and vocational, basic to higher education, means that a much wider range of subject cultures, required facilities and assessment modes are in play.

Implications for leadership

The factors above have led to differences in the history, culture, intended market and curriculum of schools, colleges and work-based learning providers, resulting in different approaches to leadership (Lumby and Briggs, 2002; Simkins, 2000). Learners and staff are aware of a different culture in schools and colleges. Fourteen to sixteen-year-old learners note the greater liberty in colleges, the more adult relationship with tutors, the loosening of structures they see as constraining, symbolized by the short periods marked by a bell (Lumby and Morrison, 2004). Similarly, learners in sixth form colleges note that one of the main reasons for not staying in the school sixth form but opting to come to a sixth form college is the greater sense of liberty (Lumby and Briggs, 2002). Staff specifically rate the culture of their college in relation to schools and general further education colleges, one end of the spectrum being identical to school culture and the other end identical to that of general further education colleges (ibid.). As perceived by both learners and staff, the teaching and learning culture of institutions varies considerably.

Equally the pressures of competition have established a different culture of leadership. There is a considerable literature on managerialism in schools and in the post-compulsory sector (Gleeson and Shain, 1999; Simkins, 2000), suggesting that financial imperatives have driven leaders to fundamental changes which have had an impact on the nature of leadership. However, the impact has been far greater in the post-compulsory sector. For example, the increasing percentage of part-time and contract staff, over 50 per cent of all staff (FEDA, 1995), has transformed the relationship between leaders and lecturers, and between core and peripheral staff (Elliott and Hall, 1994).

While leaders in different educational organizations may agree on broad aims, such as wanting to help all learners to achieve their potential, such common and acceptable statements may be a convenient way of concealing a complex set of beliefs and loyalties which do not necessarily align easily with the publicly stated intentions. In other words, the generally stated aims, as for example set out in the school or college prospectus, may be a mythology which allows everyone to feel comfortable that their purposes are selfless and equitable, but which may conceal differences between the different types of organization. They may also obscure less publicly acceptable aims, such as assuring the survival or prestige of the organization or the retention of staff, which may lie beneath the surface. The implication of the content of mission statements is that all leaders share similar educational values and aims but, in fact, the situation may be much more fragmented and varied. As an example, a survey which investigated if the use of time of middle-level leaders (heads of department) had changed since 1993, discovered that those in further education colleges spent much more time on financial issues than their counterparts in sixth form colleges, as illustrated in Figure 11.1. Whatever the heads of department concerned might say, the use of their time indicates that those in sixth from colleges are as focused on learning aims as they have historically been, and those in FE colleges have become more focused on financial issues.

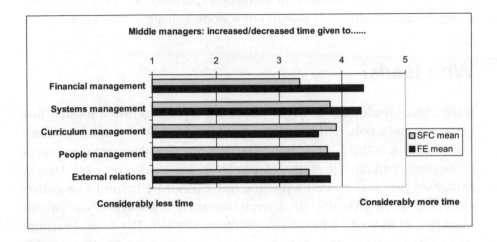

Figure 11.1
Change in use of time in further education and sixth form colleges since 1993 (Lumby and Briggs, 2002: 75)

The rhetoric about learner-centredness is also suspect. While leadership is assumed to be focused on the learner, it may in fact be primarily concerned with the organization as the unit by which effects are assessed. This book has presented a range of evidence that the best interests of the learner are set aside in favour of the interests of the organization. For example, when schools wish to maintain numbers entering the sixth form, information on other options may be withheld from learners (Foskett et al., 2004). The view of the outgoing Chair of the Learning and Skills Council is that the Strategic Area Reviews, supposedly considering what local arrangements would be in the best interests of learners, are often blocked by pressure groups, such as schools fighting to maintain their own sixth form whatever the circumstances or review indicates (Kingston, 2004). Young people may be prevented from attending vocational training at a local college if the school needs them to achieve GCSE at grade C or above. Such evidence indicates a case to be answered by leaders, that the rhetoric of putting learners first is any more than just a convenient public and professional public relations stance.

It is easy to assume that all those teaching 14–19-year-olds are 'educators' and as such share much in common. In fact those in schools, colleges and work-based learning may view their work from very different perspectives. They inhabit different worlds; consequently, assumptions about common aims and values are untenable. How, then, are leaders to secure a coherent learning experience for 14–19-year-olds as they cross the different cultures of school, college and workplace?

Who leads?

If the aim of leadership of 14–19 education is then to find a socially just pedagogy and a coherent learning experience for 14–19-year-olds, whose responsibility is this? Who leads? Local and regional strategic responsibilities are split at the point of provision for under or over 16s, as explained previously. Such a fracture line cannot be helpful to a coherent vision of 14–19 education. Even where there is a single body with an overview, as in post-16 provision, problems remain. The Local Learning and Skills Council has a duty to review provision for 16–19-year-olds within its area, and to ensure the optimum arrangement of organizations and curriculum is agreed. However, micropolitical forces exert pressure. Views on what constitutes the optimum arrangement are likely to be shaped by what is politically acceptable to the range of stakeholders, the influence of each being dependent on their power (Kingston, 2004). If any body with an overview, whether LEA, LLSC or Regional Development Agency (RDA) is constrained by the influence of stakeholders, the issue of working together to provide local education in the best interests of learners reverts in practice back to the organizations themselves. The imperative for leadership for both achievement and for social justice remains at organizational level, whatever organization is supposedly given the strategic overview and responsibility.

The vehicle often suggested for organizations to achieve coherence is partnership. Chapter 9 reviewed the progress made in establishing partnerships and the difficulties which exist in making them work in what remains a competitive environment. Partnerships are so often 'a series of chancy, short-lived, and often merely paper exercises in hope' (Griffiths, 2000, p. 394), rather than a realistic way of deconstructing barriers. Given the underlying differences in culture and approach between many 14–19 providers, partnership is not a panacea, but a challenge which remains deeply problematic. The concept of partnership begs the question of who is to lead partnerships. Are colleges to take the lead, or schools, or is a genuine distribution of leadership possible and desirable?

How is leadership to be enacted?

Raffe (2002) notes that government strategy is consistently to make changes to the supply side of education, changing the curriculum, qualifications, the structure of providers' institutions. It has not made any concerted effort to tackle the demand side. Consequently, what is demanded by learners, parents and employers has remained largely stable, and schools and colleges have by and large responded by providing what is wanted, not necessarily needed, in order to survive. Leaders in schools, colleges and work-based learning have been squeezed between a government fixated on raising achievement figures and individuals and their families who want to achieve what the culture within which they live will see as 'success'. For middle-class families, maintaining or increasing their status is a profound compulsion (Reay, 2001a). Education for them is primarily a means of maintaining or increasing social capital, not for producing an equal society. For working-class families, education may be seen as an escape from one status to another, or as a means of fulfilling potential, or as an irrelevance (ibid.). On all sides eroding inequalities, achieving real change may not be the aim. Rather, maintaining a differentiated system with differentiated outcomes, in terms of pathways and related status, may be the preference. Nor are educators neutral parties. They are likely to value more the path which has led to their own success, and they are also likely to favour developments which benefit them personally and/or their institution. The field is intensely political and riven with conflict and turf wars.

The emphasis in much of the analysis and development of leadership at the end of the twentieth and start of the twenty-first centuries has been a focus on learning. The failure of 14–19 education, with entrenched positions, interests and resulting advantage/disadvantage to groups of young people, suggests a different focus is needed. Leaders need to focus on moral and political purposes. We have argued that leadership for 14–19-year-olds is about finding a socially just pedagogy. The achievement of this is dependent not so much on skills of teaching and learning, but on political skills to work with others, to change opinions, to take risks and above all, to review one's own moral position and to challenge others to do the same. Fourteen to nineteen education has not let down many young people because the curriculum and qualifications structure was not right, but because of the attitudes which underpin the decisions made about changes in curriculum and qualifications.

The needs of 14–19-year-olds challenge leaders to move from a tunnel vision in their own organization, to see learning holistically across young people's lives and across organizations; they also require a vision which is about young people's life outcomes, not just their qualification results at 16 or 19, or any other age. Leadership needs to move from a focus on 'learning' so often a euphemism for credentialism, to a focus on the impetus for which many came into education, to offer life chances to the young and to look to their moral, spiritual, cultural and intellectual growth. If this sounds utopian, that is because it is. There is an argument that changing behaviour will change attitudes, not vice versa. But changing behaviour through changing the national structures of oversight, curricula and qualifications has a long history of not working. The alternative strategy of trying to change attitudes, attacking the demand side, remains the alternative. Unless leaders can lift their heads in this way, and lead the community to a broader view of the purpose of 14–19 education and how it might be achieved, young people will remain locked into the age-old system which fails so many.

Reality check

The first task is for leaders to review their own values. Swift argued that satire is like a mirror in which people see everyone's face except their own. This could equally be applied to analyses of inequity. Leaders of 14–19 education are unlikely to implicate themselves in the causes of social injustice, locating the problem elsewhere. Delving too deeply into the hidden rather than the overt curriculum is not fashionable. The role of the leader in education and training is, then, to work with others in their organization and, critically, across other organizations to acknowledge how their curriculum, pedagogy, attitudes and practice may be contributing to the continuation of inequity and underachievement. No amount of review of the curriculum or changes in policy at national level will seriously dent existing divisions and disadvantages to learners without a challenge to values, beliefs and aims at the local and organizational level. Without such a fundamental rethinking, moving around the curriculum and accreditation pieces is in danger of replacing one mythology with another. This is the central challenge of leadership for 14–19.

Who, then, will rise to this challenge? The experience of leaders is currently limited. Schools are concerned with the full 14–19 age range, but generally not the full attainment range at 16–19, and their curriculum is far more limited than that of colleges. Leaders in the Learning and Skills Sector have experience of a very wide curriculum including academic courses, but generally for 16–19-year-olds. On the face of it, neither has the experience to truly lead a coherent 14–19 education. However, college leaders are catching up as their experience of 14–16-year-olds grows. School leaders, for their part, are attempting to expand their curriculum to encompass a wider range of vocational programmes. Schools are increasingly aware that colleges have the potential to seriously erode their 14–19 market. The preference of many 14–19-year-olds for the more adult environment and greater facilities of colleges presents, in the words of one college Key Stage 4 co-ordinator, 'a bit of a wake up call for schools' (Lumby and Morrison, 2004, p. 41). It is not inconceivable to imagine a future scenario where independent 11–18 schools offer the major alternative to 14–19 education in general further education colleges, with maintained schools squeezed out.

The possible future models are then for leaders from both schools and the Learning and Skills Sector to act in partnership, or for one or the other to take the overall lead in shaping and offering 14–19 education. At this point in time, the history of competition and unsatisfactory partnership arrangements suggest one or the other becoming dominant as a more likely future scenario. It is interesting to speculate whether the moral and pedagogic imperatives will compel partnership in the face of continuing competition or, if not, which group one might put money on to emerge as the new leaders of 14–19 education.

PART 4

FUTURES

Chapter 12

Future policy 14–19: choices and visions

Our journey within this book has explored in detail the emergence and current status of the key components of education and training 14–19, including the curriculum, the experiences of learners and the way the system is organized and managed. In this final chapter we step back to focus on the big picture, which is the world that policy-makers inhabit, and undertake the two tasks essential for policy leaders – identifying the major themes, issues and perspectives in 14–19, and drawing out the key choices faced at national level. This perspective on policy choices is built around five key themes – themes that we believe address not just operational matters but also fundamental issues of equity, opportunity and professionalism. While the choices must be made at a political level, the forces for change can emanate from all those with a stake in the education and training of 14–19-year-olds, not least the young people themselves – the issues are for all of us engaged in 14–19 to reflect on.

14–19 retrospect

So what is the big picture in 14–19? From our analysis there are five themes that we think are fundamental in understanding the current nature of 14–19:

1. Turbulence masquerading as change.
2. The dominance of assessment and classification and the primacy of academic pathways.
3. Alternative strategies for change.
4. The confused environment of 14–19 provision and choice.
5. The absence of student voice.

We shall examine each below.

Turbulence masquerading as change

Across the whole of the education arena in England the period since James Callaghan's Ruskin Speech in 1976 has been portrayed as one of rapid, continuous and fundamental change. A student who left an FE college in 1975, or a secondary school headteacher who retired then, could certainly comment at length on the differences between then and now. Each of our chapters illustrates how change is endemic. We have argued, though, that this change is simply turbulence, a reworking and realignment of the surface of the ocean that has made little difference to the underlying pattern of currents and tides.

This is best illustrated with reference to the curriculum. In 1975 the curriculum for all young people after the age of 14 was but a modified form of a century-old academic programme, and the majority of those who proceeded with their education beyond 16 did so in institutions with an academic ethos and a primary aim of achieving university entrance for their students. Despite the rhetoric of vocationalizing the curriculum, a higher proportion of young people now spend their post-16 education in a classroom environment than in 1976. In part, of course, it is the marketization of the sector that has produced this effect. While choice was envisaged as giving young people the chance to choose more widely, it is the market value of academic qualifications and university entrance that have persuaded them (and their parents) that this narrow set of choices actually represents the best return on their investment.

Similarly, the predominant approaches to learning are still centred on the teacher as knowledge source. The teaching room of 2004 is very similar to the classroom or workshop of 1976 and, indeed, the instigation of a ladder of assessment with more rungs in it has pushed many teachers towards, rather than away from, more conservative teaching styles, with the priority of syllabus coverage driven by the imperative of high examination grades for their students (and their institution).

If the policy intent was fundamental change but the result was merely turbulence, we must ask why this has been so. In part it may be attributed to the rapidity of change itself. From 1976 onwards initiative followed initiative as politicians and their advisers generated yet more interesting proposals, reflecting the desire of each government and each quango to pursue its own individual priorities, and an impatience based on the political necessity to see 'impact' long before the system could actually deliver it. In such cases short-term limited achievement is often interpreted as failure, or a new and different idea is thought likely to deliver change more quickly. Whatever the cause, innovation overload inevitably resulted in the failure of the majority of the initiatives to deliver anything other than surface change. Furthermore, expectation of further change in short order inevitably reduces the commitment of implementers to any single initiative – next month/year will bring along a different demand for change. Change that is too rapid almost inevitably is doomed to have limited impact.

The dominance of assessment, classification and academic pathways

We must also recognize the embeddedness of the cultural values that are represented in our education and training system. The systems that have emerged in England over two centuries are not chance developments. They represent views of the nature and purpose of education and training, and are imbued with a set of values that are very deep rooted. Central is a view that high-status education is about academic learning, within which is transmitted important cultural and societal knowledge between genera- tions. It is those individuals who can demonstrate expertise in such learning who are able to aspire to positions of economic or political power.

We can also identify the persistent vision of 14–19 education and training as a phase of classification and sorting of young people into the academic sheep and the vocational goats. Assessment and classification drive the curriculum and drive the organizational structures within insti- tutions. Indeed, a component of the 14–19 system is the sorting of institutions themselves into those which are successful and those which are less so, where success is measured principally by academic achieve- ment. In a culture of delegating blame to institutions, woe betide the school or college which is classified as a low achiever by the public judgement of the league tables.

Linked to this is the belief that the nature of knowledge and the defi- nition of what is important knowledge is derived not from within society but from within the university sector, so that the pre-19 curriculum is driven by the needs of higher education. It is the universities rather than any particular school examination which are the most fundamental element of the English education system, and A levels are important as they represent the traditional access route to higher education. In the political skirmishes about the nature and organization of education it is the universities who hold the cultural power, hence it will be schools and colleges where change is more likely to be demanded.

The power of the universities represents the strength of key institutions, and their conservative nature in English society. This is true, also, of the school system itself, for the nature, organization and values of schools are much the same now as they were a century ago. It is in the interests of the existing organizations to make change only slowly when their key value as measured by society as a whole is in the traditional systems, methods and values that they apply. Resistance to fundamental change, therefore, is endemic. This is not a uniquely English problem, however, for the values and history we have described here are those of western societies more broadly. While the detail varies between states, western societies generally have education systems driven by the academic values of universities, and school systems which emphasize objectives-based education and deficit models of learning and assessment rather than developmental models of education. Education is about the replication of society and about classification and selection. As such it has an important element of social ritual within it, and we can regard the education and training system as providing the ritual processes for young people to progress from childhood to the adult environment of the economy and the world of work. Rituals of assessing achievement and ability and of enabling young people to find their niche in society are writ large within the 14–19 sector. Examinations and applications are important rituals in themselves, both symbolizing and functioning as the transition to adult life. Changing the rituals of society and changing the need for ritual is intensely challenging for government, and may in part explain the limited fundamental change that we can observe in the 14–19 sector.

Alternative strategies for change

Despite the limitations of fundamental change, it is clear that the last quarter century has been characterized by strategies for change by government in relation to 14–19. We have identified how change has been promoted in three key waves: the use of agencies and funded initiatives, principally a feature of the 1980s; the use of structural change with the promotion of self-managing institutions and market processes, principally in the late 1980s and early 1990s; and the use of curriculum change, commencing with the arrival of GCSEs in the late 1980s and still continuing with the proposals for reform emerging from the Tomlinson Report (Working Group on 14–19 Reform, 2004). This pattern of change has two characteristics that are significant.

First, it exemplifies well what Dass and Parker (1999) have described as episodic change, when periods of change occur after periods of policy stability in response to necessity and opportunity rather than long-term strategy. We might see the post-1976 period as one such episode, initiated by the view that economic stress and youth unemployment required government to do *something*, or we might equally characterize it as a sequence of merged episodes. Such episodes historically occur at the end of periods of economic crisis and are a response to seek to avoid the circumstances in which such crisis can re-emerge or have the same economic consequences. Such periods of change demand significant reworking of operational systems and make substantial demands on those within the service. Often, however, they result in less embedding of the features of change than the change that emerges from within the system itself (what Dass and Parker [1999] term 'systemic change'), when the change is in accordance with the evolving values of those working in education (Fullan, 2003).

Secondly there has been a contradiction between the rhetoric and reality of the focus of change. The rhetoric has emphasized the importance of the demand side of the education and training system. This is illustrated through the prioritization of choice for young people (and parents) and the central influence given to the business community, which is another prioritized consumer of the outputs of education and training. The policy reality, though, has been the continuous adjustment of the supply side of the system, with each of the three waves of change identified above focusing on a specific aspect of that supply side. In practice, changing the demand side is much more problematic since, ultimately, it can be achieved only by manipulating choice. The use of funding models, curriculum change, inspection and public accountability through the use of league tables have all in effect constrained the choice of young people while at the same time promoting choice as the essence of the new system.

The confused environment of 14–19 provision and choice

Emerging from this episode of change, therefore, has been an environment for 14–19 that has been characterized by confusion, contradiction, conflict and intensity. These characteristics have been observable from the perspective of those working in and leading 14–19 and also by the young people working through school, college and training (and by their parents, families and advisers). Confusion has arisen from the rapidity of operational change, its often short-term persistence and the fact that complexity and increases in choice have been an important consequence. Seeking to answer an obvious and basic question for a 14/15-year-old, such as 'what choices are available to me at 16?', has become much more difficult as the number of pathways, programmes and institutions has increased and where new initiatives come and go over short timescales (for example, CPVE and National Traineeships). Contradiction is characterized by the outcomes of different policy initiatives from the government. This is perhaps an inevitable consequence of policy and strategy being derived from a range of government departments and quangos, but creates significant tensions and ambiguities for organizations and for young people. This issue is illustrated well by the contradictions between policy that promotes the development of vocational pathways through 16–19 education and policy that encourages universities to still value academic A levels as the primary currency of HE entrance. Conflict has emerged as a consequence of competition in education and training markets, where institutions are encouraged to adopt competitive relationships with other providers in their locality at the expense of collaborative ones. Conflict from competition is itself, too, an example of contradiction, in that the emphasis in government policy on regional collaboration contrasts markedly with the reality of competition on the ground.

Finally, the turbulence of the 14–19 sector has generated an environment that is much more intense for both institutions and young people. For institutions, that intensity has arisen from both the rapidity with which change has been demanded and the relatively new demand to engage with the external environment of both the marketplace and the pressure for partnership and collaboration. Scanning, sensing and responding to the external environment (Hanson and Henry, 1992) are demanding of both financial and time resources. The increase in workload and stress amongst teachers and managers reported from within schools and colleges would seem to be symptomatic of this intensity.

For young people, the intensity arises from the increased frequency of assessment and the consequent increase in the frequency of choice decisions. At the end of the 1970s young people experienced public examinations at the end of year 11 and, if they stayed on to study A levels, year 13. By 2004 public examinations occur in year 9 (SATs), year 11, year 12 and year 13, so the exposure of young people to high-stakes assessment has increased significantly. And each assessment period is followed immediately by a moment of choice about what pathway and subjects to follow for the subsequent assessment period. Choice gives flexibility but also adds pressure and intensity to young people's lives.

The absence of student voice

In concluding this retrospect we must recognize the relative disenfranchisement of young people within the system. The rhetoric of choice and learner-centred education and training is loud, yet the reality is that the voice of young people has not been an important element in the review and development of policy and practice. The system emphasizes their acquisition of knowledge and skills for the economy but places relatively little emphasis on their development as individuals across the full gamut of human characteristics. This is of particular significance since 14–19 is possibly the most important period of personal development for young people in the whole of their lives. As long as a key policy question is 'What does society want from the education of 14–19 year olds?' rather than 'What are the needs of 14–19 year olds within an education and training system?' then the organization and systems in place will largely be something that is done *to* young people rather than done *for* them.

14–19 futures

So what is the future in the 14–19 arena? The emergence of 14–19 as a single sector of the education and training system that needs planning in an integrated way is a strong feature of government policy (DfES, 2004b). In reflecting on how the sector might change towards such a vision we have identified six fundamental themes that address essential aspects of any future system and act as a framework for policy development. Although presented as separate themes, they are inevitably intimately connected. We now provide some perspectives on what shape these themes should take in the future.

Learners must be 'at the centre'

Within the 14–19 sector the number of vested interests is large. The government, employers, higher education, schools, colleges, young people and parents are but part of the list of actively engaged and interested parties. Each has its own distinct priorities, but whose priorities are the most important? The simple answer, of course, is that there must be a balance, with a focus on those priorities that serve the interests of most of the stakeholders. At present the agenda is driven by government economic priorities and the recruitment agendas of universities. As a result, the priorities of young people themselves are often being marginalized. We must consider, therefore, how to redress the balance of power in identifying priorities and how to ensure that the voice of young people is heard in debates about future policy and practice. The cost of not doing so will be the persistence of a narrow academic curriculum, inappropriate for most young people, and the continuing emphasis on assessment and selection as key motivators within the sector. More significant, though, will be increasing detachment between the education and training context and the real lives and needs of young people, raising important issues of social equity and significant risks of seeing the persistence of current patterns of social exclusion and associated social problems.

A key issue within this theme, therefore, is about how we balance the social aims of 'success for all' and 'inclusion' with the needs of society and the economy for the classification and selection of young people. Both are important aims, and the priority between them will reflect individual political ideology. But if social inclusion is a real political priority then the increasing role of education and training in selecting and classifying will need to be reduced in emphasis, and both assessment systems and the curriculum need fundamental review.

Employers need to 'get real'

The role of employers and business within the 14–19 phase has been an important priority since the expansion of the MSC in the 1970s and 1980s. Two consistent but contradictory messages have been presented from employers. On the one hand, they contend that the education/

training system needs to address the shortfall in both core/key skills and the numbers of young people engaged in vocational training (CBI, 1989). On the other, the primacy of A levels and a narrowly based academic curriculum is stressed as the gold standard for those seeking to enter employment or higher education at 18. We have shown in Chapter 5 how the changing nature of work and careers makes such distinctions inappropriate and counter-productive.

In both perspectives, though, there is an assumption that the education and training system is there to deliver 'just-in-time' trained employees, and that the role of employers and business in training and development is limited. Reviews of attitudes amongst OECD countries shows clearly the relatively low investment by UK business in training (DfES, 2003e). There is a strong need, therefore, to recognize that public sector education and training cannot deliver the diverse and specific needs of business either with the precision or within the time parameters of responsiveness that business would ideally like. If the system cannot meet employer expectations, then employers must scale down their expectations and scale up their own role in training and development. Recognition of this need is clear in the government's Skills Strategy (DfES, 2003e), which emphasizes the role of the 23 new Sector Skills Councils. Despite this rhetoric, though, there is still a sense in which training is seen as the individual's responsibility alone rather than also as the employer's. If employers did both scale down their expectation of education and scale up their own commitment to undertake a more active role in training, this would have the advantage of increasing investment in training throughout the economy and ensure the specific needs of employers are met more precisely. It would also reduce the culture of blame in relation to education and training about failing to meet economic needs, and enable education and training to focus on the generic operational, intellectual, decision-making and learning skills that are of value across the economy and society.

Recognize that partnership and competition are incompatible

Fourteen to nineteen education and training engages in some way almost every player within the economy and society, and the rhetoric of partnership is strong within the sector. We have seen through our analysis in Chapter 10, however, that the reality of partnership is only poorly developed, and the guarded relationships promoted by highly competitive environments militate against effective partnership. The two appear to be mutually exclusive because of their opposed aims, so policy-makers must decide between them and not equivocate through the rhetoric that both are achievable.

Despite its limited development, we believe that partnership is essential if the key focus within the sector is to be the needs of young people, since these are so diverse that it is inconceivable they can be met by a single organization working in isolation. The biggest partnership challenge is about connections across the age 16 'divide', where the cultures and histories of school education and post-16 education and training come into contact. Only through joint planning within local contexts will the learning necessary by individuals and organizations on either side of the boundary be achieved. The evidence from the evaluation of 14–19 Pathfinder projects (Lumby and Morrison, 2004) provides exciting evidence that such joint planning is achievable and that the benefits that accrue to young people from this are substantial

Recognize that 'choice' is a two-edged sword

The premise of enhanced choice has underwritten most of the policy initiatives of government since 1980. We have identified in Chapter 8, however, that choice represents a complex and demanding challenge for most young people. Furthermore, it is not clear that choice has increased in all dimensions, for while there are clearly more programmes and more providers at all levels between 14 and 19 than there were 25 years ago, we have seen a convergence in the range of choices rather than divergence. In the language of the market we have seen increased subdivision of the main market segments rather than the creation of new ones.

And just how real is choice? For many young people, frequently those from professional middle-class backgrounds, the choice is narrow, for the only choice with market value is to pursue academic programmes towards university entrance. At the other extreme is the frequently bewildering choice of academic, vocational or training programmes faced by those who are from less academically achieving, often working-class, backgrounds. The choice is wide, but the range of support from parents and professional services is highly variable, and for some the response to complexity is to disengage from choice, or pursue the line of least resistance that reflects dominant cultural norms within their own socio-economic context. Hence the consequence is a replication of the decisions of family or friends.

We must also consider the impact of choice, a right that is proclaimed from most corners of the political ring, and in particular the appropriateness of delegating such a significant responsibility to young people themselves. Young people are by definition both inexperienced choosers and inexperienced in their understanding of society in general and the labour market in particular. Is it right that we confront them with choice that can be quite so significant in its implications across their lifetime? We have two responses to this dilemma. First, we could seek to increase young people's understanding of risk, of decision-making, and of the choices open to them and their implications. In many ways this is what careers education and guidance and the work of the Connexions service seeks to do, but there is ample evidence of the enormity of this task (for example, Lumby et al., 2003). Secondly, we could reduce the complexity and range of choice by moving towards a more common curriculum that is appropriate to most young people irrespective of their ultimate destination. Such is the proposal for the 'core' element of the proposals emerging from the Tomlinson Report (Working Group on 14–19 Reform, 2003).

Retreat from assessment, focus on teaching young people to learn and reform the higher education admissions systems

Before we can build an appropriate 14–19 education and training system we have to decide what young people should learn, and what learning and teaching should look like. The traditional curriculum divide between academic and vocational pathways has been dogged with deep-seated issues of the lack of parity of esteem. Such barriers of status are difficult to break down – they appear to be almost universal 'truths'. Similarly, traditional pedagogies seem fundamentally resistant to change in the context of assessment-intense curricula. If we cannot break down these traditions we must either live with their effects in replicating social structures and divisions, or look for an alternative approach to curriculum and pedagogy.

What should this alternative look like? A socially just curriculum might include a common core of knowledge and skills for all, that runs throughout the 14–19 phase, in addition to which, individuals might choose to add specialist fields that reflect their interests, abilities and ambitions, and this is the model proposed initially by Tomlinson (Working Group on 14–19 Reform, 2003). Tomlinson has suggested a balanced curriculum in which:

> All 14–19 year olds should follow programmes of learning which contain a balance of: the general skills and knowledge which everybody needs for adult life and to undertake further learning and employment ... specialist learning, such as specific academic and vocational knowledge and skills ... (and) supplementary learning which will help support their progress ... Young people should work towards a high status diploma qualification covering the whole of their learning programme ... . (Working Group on 14–19 Reform, 2003, p. 4)

While such an approach moves towards a breakdown of some of the socially divisive elements of the existing curriculum, it still retains assessment as its primary shaper, which in itself may drive the replication of existing learning and teaching approaches. It is unrealistic to see the 14–19 education and training system not fulfilling societal needs for assessment of young people's skills and capabilities, but that assessment can be less intensive. Our new curriculum 14–19 must prioritize learning over assessment.

An important driver in the curriculum is the issue of higher education entry. It is beyond the scope of this volume to review and critique the nature and organization of HE, but it is equally clear that the current HE admissions system and the emphasis on performance indicators based on admissions rather than outcomes of HE will cause universities and colleges to find selection criteria within *any* 14–19 assessment system. The key to changing the values within the 14–19 curriculum, therefore, lies principally in HE admissions and selections systems. This must be a priority for review if the 14–19 curriculum is to be freed from the shackles of high-stakes assessment and narrow approaches to learning.

Loosen the coupling between 14–19 funding and student numbers

Within any public service the funding system acts not only as a mechanism for acquiring resources but also as an indicator of priorities for organizational and operational choices. The funding models used by FEFC and, more recently, the LSC have, for example, emphasized student retention and achievement, and have also encouraged expansion of the sector by reducing the unit of resource. In deciding the funding model that is most appropriate, therefore, we need to know how we respond to each of the previous themes – they define the sort of system we are seeking to produce

Existing models prioritize choice and the funding of individual learners by linking income in a direct way to student numbers. In this way learners become a commodity for institutions, and the culture is strongly that of competition, the market and student choice. We have seen throughout this book how such an approach emphasizes the primacy of a small subset of choices, but also implicates institutions in persuading young people to make choices that are in the institution's, rather than the individual learner's, interests (Foskett et al., 2004).

The alternative is to adopt a funding model which funds institutions to provide a range of programmes but where the flow of finance is much less directly connected to current student numbers. Such models functioned prior to FE incorporation in 1992, and were criticized for encouraging complacency and less concern with standards and achievements by learners. While this was certainly the case, the benefits came in two important areas. Funding was predictable in the medium term, and so encouraged a longer-term perspective within the organization, and also enabled colleges to place a greater emphasis on the development needs of the individual.

The constraints of public finance and the demand for public accountability of the education/training service makes a return to earlier funding models difficult to achieve in the current political climate. It is a challenging concept because it requires professional trust, for institutions to be allowed to develop the most appropriate response to local needs, and social and economic priorities. However, a model that balances the positive dimensions of the two approaches might be explored for the future. In this way the stability of funding for institutions that comes from a longer-term view and reduced competition can be balanced with the benefits of a concern for quality and standards and responsiveness to outside communities that comes with a per capita funding model.

14–19 towards 2020

These six themes provide a framework for shaping the emerging 14–19 sector. Moynagh and Worsley (2003) present a number of scenarios for the future of the post-16 sector in the UK, as part of the Tomorrow Project, a scenario-building exercise across all public sector fields. They observe that the shape of the future is dependent on how far government chooses to increase or decrease central regulation and increase or maintain current levels of investment in the sector. Such decisions reflect the political ideologies of particular governments, but it seems most likely that the 'steady as she goes' scenario of strong central regulation and current levels of funding is the most likely future.

Whichever scenario emerges as reality, however, there are a number of areas of development that our analysis show to be important. First, the importance of professionalism, as a vehicle for leading the sector and innovating in ways that meet the balanced needs of young people and society, is paramount. Building on the professional knowledge and expertise of the wide range of agencies and stakeholders involved in the sector is critical, and we would strongly support the government rhetoric of partnership. But partnership requires professionalism and trust, not competition and independence, and professionalism needs to be actively promoted by government and by professional bodies. Professionalism, of course, entails working primarily in the interests of young people and not just with self-interest or in the interests of the organization, and those working in education and training will need to demonstrate that they can respond to this challenge. The last two decades have seen a strong shift away from this aspect of professionalism, so this is a trend that will need to be reversed, but our observation of 14–19 Pathfinder projects suggests that the professional will is there. This leads to the second of our priorities, which is the drawing back from the frontiers of competition and the market. The market is often an effective resource allocation system but, where strong competition is the result, this has a negative impact on some of the other keys to success, notably partnership between institutions, equity between young people, and social justice. Thirdly, the focus needs to shift from young people as commodities to young people as individuals with their own development needs. Providing mechanisms for them to progress from 14 to 19 with appropriate choices, but protected from the most threatening and stressful elements of being a consumer, will be an important challenge for the system. The development of Individual Learning Plans is a promising start to this.

The commitment of government to establishing a distinctive 14–19 sector in England has been made explicit through a range of policy documents since 1997. We have explored within this book the logic of a 14–19 sector and have shown that it provides a clear connection between the education, training and personal development needs of young people. Young people post-14 are very different to those pre-14 in terms of their needs and focus, with a clear transition from schoolchild to young adult. The challenge is that such a model requires a substantial adjustment in a system in which the natural break has been at 16, despite the fact that in effect the 'formal education leaving age' has now been raised from 16 to 18. Bringing together schools, colleges, training organizations and other stakeholders to engage with the culture, values and systems on the other side of the divide at 16 requires a large investment of time, goodwill and commitment. The sector will not emerge because government says it should but because it is the most appropriate natural fit to young people's needs – and even that will happen only if the inertia and friction in existing organizational arrangements can be overcome, and the voice of young people and the professionalism of staff are central to the vision. Such a vision is shared by many of the current leaders of institutions in the sector:

> [I]t's all very well asking principals what they think, but colleges don't belong to principals. Colleges belong to the students and staff who study and work in them. The main thing they want is that colleges are good places to learn and good places to work … It will be a measure of their eventual success that this, in fact, is what happens.
> (Thomson, 2004, p. 17)

We believe that we have arrived at a key period of opportunity in the development of education and training, where a strong 14–19 sector can emerge that delivers a high-quality experience that is primarily in the interests of young people rather than all the other stakeholders. If our six themes are addressed, some of the persistent nettles within English education and training will have been grasped and we would be confident that our vision for our 14–19-year-olds will be much closer to realization. We have argued in this book that getting it right for 14–19-year-olds has implications for all of us, that the hopes of making our society both more inclusive and more just, on the one hand, and more economically productive, on the other, hinge on this phase of education. If the opportunities are not grasped, if the English disease of radical rhetoric outweighed by conservative cultures persists, then young adults will continue to find themselves the victims of the system rather than the principal clients of it. The danger for us all will then lie in the corrosive divisions that post-14 education and training currently creates and consolidates for society. Failure will come to haunt not just young people, but all of us.

References

Ahier, J. and Ross, A. (1995) *The Social Subjects within the Curriculum*, London, Falmer Press.

Ainley, P. (1990) *Vocational Education and Training*, London, Cassell.

Apple, M. (2004) 'Cultural politics and the text', in Ball. S. (ed.) *Sociology of Education*, London, RoutledgeFalmer.

Armitage, A., Bryant, B., Dunhill, R., Hammersley, M., Hayes, D., Hudson, A. and Lawes, S. (1999) *Teaching and Training in Post-Compulsory Education*, Buckingham, Open University Press.

Ashworth, L. (1995) *Children's Voices in School Matters*, London, ACE Ltd.

Assessment and Learning Research Synthesis Group (2002) 'A systematic review of the impact of summative assessment and test on students' motivation for learning', London, EPPI-Centre, accessed online January 2004, http://eppi.ioe.ac.uk/EPPIWebContent/reel/review_groups/assessment/ass_rv1/ass_rv1.pdf

Audit Commission/OFSTED (1993) *Unfinished Business: Full-time Educational Courses for 16–19 year olds. A Study by the Audit Commission and HMI*, London, HMSO.

Baldwin, J. (2003) 'The management styles of further education managers during rapid and extensive change – a case study', unpublished PhD thesis, University of Nottingham.

Ball, S. (1999) 'Industrial training or new vocationalism? Structures and discourses', in Flude, M. and Sieminski, S. (eds) *Education, Training and the Future of Work II. Developments in Vocational Education and Training*, London, Routledge in association with the Open University.

Ball, S. (2003) *Class Strategies and the Education Market*, London, RoutledgeFalmer.

Ball, S.J., Maguire, M. and MacRae, S. (2001) *Choice Pathways and Transitions: 16–19 Education, Training and (Un)Employment in One Urban Locale*, Swindon, ESRC.

Bates, I. (1998) 'The empowerment dimension in GNVQs', *Evaluation and Research in Education*, vol. 2, no. 1, pp. 7–22.

Bates, I. (2002) *Problematizing Empowerment in Education and Work: An Exploration of GNVQ*, Leeds, School of Education.

Becker, G.S. (1975) *Human Capital: A Theoretical and Empirical Analysis with Special Reference to Education*, New York, Columbia University Press.

Belfield, C., Bullock, A., Rikowski, G. and Thomas, H. (nd) *Funding for the Future: Strategic Research in Further Education*, Birmingham, University of Birmingham.

Bennett, N., Harvey, J. and Anderson, L. (2004) 'Control, autonomy and partnership in local education', *Educational Management Administration and Leadership*, vol. 32, no. 2, pp. 217–35.

Bentley, T. (1998) *Learning Beyond the Classroom: Education for a Changing World*, London, Routledge.

Bernstein, B. (1977) *Class Codes and Control*, London, Routledge.

Black, P. (1993) 'Formative and summative assessment by teachers', *Studies in Science Education*, vol. 21, pp. 49–97.

Black, P. and William, D. (1998) 'Assessment and classroom learning', *Assessment in Education: Principles, Policy and Practice*, vol. 5, no. 1, pp. 7–75, accessed

online 19 December 2003,
http://search.epnet.com/direct.asp?an=725610&db=afh

Blatchford, P. (1996) 'Pupils' views on school work and school from 7–16 years', *Research Papers in Education*, vol. 11, no. 3, pp. 263–88.

Bloomer, M. (1998) '"They tell you what to do and then they let you get on with it": the illusion of progressivism in GNVQ', *Journal of Education and Work*, vol. 11, no. 2, pp. 167–86.

Bolton, T. and Hyland, T. (2003) 'Implementing key skills in further education: perceptions and issues', *Journal of Further and Higher Education*, vol 27, no. 1, pp. 15–26.

Bond, C. (1993) 'Flexible learning – a conceptual framework', *Training Officer*, vol. 29, no. 6, pp. 166–8.

Bottery, M. (2002) 'The management and mismanagement of trust', paper presented at the British Educational Leadership and Management Association Annual Conference, Birmingham, 20–22 September 2002.

Bourdieu, P. (1993) ' Postscript', in Bourdieu, P. and Wacquant, L. (1992) *An Invitation to Reflexive Sociology*, Oxford, Polity Press.

Bowring-Carr, C. and West-Burnham, J. (1997) *Effective Learning in Schools*, London, Pitman.

Boyd, B. (1997) 'The statutory years of secondary education: change and progress', in Clark, M. and Munn, P. (eds) *Education in Scotland: A Policy and Practice from Pre-school to Secondary*, London, Routledge.

Briggs, A.R.J. (1999) 'Open doors? Modelling accessibility of learning resource facilities', *Journal of Further and Higher Education*, vol. 23, no. 3 pp. 317–27.

Broadfoot, P. (1998) 'Records of achievement and the learning society: a tale of two discourses', *Assessment in Education: Principles, Policy and Practice*, vol. 5, no. 3 pp. 447–78, accessed online 19 December 2003, http://search.epnet.com/direct.asp?an=1341652&db=afh

Bryson, V. (1999) *Feminist Debates: Issues of Theory and Practice*, Basingstoke, Palgrave.

Burke, J. (1995) 'Theoretical issues in relation to Jessup's Outcomes Model', in Burke, J. (ed.) *Outcomes, Learning and the Curriculum*, London, Falmer.

Bush, T. and Glover, D. (2003) *School Leadership: Concepts and Evidence*, Nottingham, NCSL.

Butterfield, S. (1998) 'Conditions for choice? The context for implementation of curricular pathways in the curriculum, 14–19, in England and Wales', *Cambridge Journal of Education*, vol. 28, no. 1 pp. 9–20.

Callaghan, J. (1976) 'The Ruskin College Speech, 18th October 1976', in Ahier, J., Cosin, B. and Hales, M. (eds) *Diversity and Change: Education Policy and Selection*, London, Routledge.

Cameron, J. and Pierce, D.P. (1994) 'Reinforcement, reward, and intrinsic motivation: a meta-analysis', *Review of Educational Research*, vol. 64, pp. 363–423.

Cantor, L., Roberts, I. and Pratley, B. (1995) *A Guide to Further Education in England and Wales*, London, Cassell.

Chapman, D. and Adams, D. (1998) 'The management and administration of education across Asia: changing challenges', *International Journal of Educational Research*, vol. 29, pp. 603–26.

Chitty, C. (1996) 'The changing role of the state in education provision', in Ahier, J., Cosin, B. and Hales, M. (eds) *Diversity and Change: Education Policy and Selec-*

tion, London, Routledge.

Cockett, M. (1996) 'Vocationalism and vocational courses 14–16', in Halsall, R. and Cockett, M. (eds) *Education and Training 14–19: Chaos or Coherence?*, London, David Fulton.

Cockett, M. and Callaghan, J. (1996) 'Caught in the middle – transition at 16+', in Halsall, R. and Cockett, M. (eds) *Education and Training 14–19: Chaos or Coherence?*, London, David Fulton.

Coffey, D. (1992) *Schools and Work: Developments in Vocational Education*, London, Cassell.

Colley, H., Hodkinson, P. and Malcolm, J. (2003) *Informality and Formality in Learning: A Report for the Learning and Skills Research Centre*, London, LSRC.

Confederation of British Industry (CBI) (1989) *Towards a Skills Revolution: A Youth Charter*, London, CBI.

Confederation of British Industry (CBI) (2002a) *The CBI Response to the Government's Green Paper '14–19: Extending Opportunities, Raising Standards'*, London, CBI.

Confederation of British Industry (CBI) (2002b) *Employment Trends Survey*, London, CBI.

Costley, D. (1996) 'Making pupils fit the framework: research into the implementation of the National Curriculum in schools for pupils with moderate learning difficulties, focusing on Key Stage 4', *School Organisation*, vol. 16, no. 3, pp. 341–54.

Crooks, T. (1998) 'The impact of classroom evaluation practices on students', *Review of Educational Research*, vol, 58, pp. 438–81.

Crowther, G. (1960) *15–18: A Report*, Central Advisory Council for Education (England).

Cuban, L. (1993) 'Computers meet classroom: classroom wins', *Teachers College Record*, vol. 95, no. 2, pp. 1–20, accessed online 3 May 2004, http://search.epnet.com/direct.asp

Dass, P. and Parker, B. (1999) 'Strategies for managing human resource diversity: from resistance to learning', *Academy of Management Executive*, vol. 13, no. 2, pp. 68–80.

Davenport, J. (1993) 'Is there any way out of the androgogy morass?', in Thorpe, M. and Edwards, R. (eds) *Culture and Processes of Adult Learning*, London, Routledge.

Davies, P. (1993) *Towards Parity of Esteem? Marketing GNVQs*, Blagdon, The Staff College.

De Pear, S. (1997) 'Excluded pupils' views of their educational needs and experience', *Support for Learning*, vol. 12, no. 2, pp. 19–22.

Dearing, R. (1996) *Review of Qualifications for 16–19 Year Olds*, London, HMSO.

Department for Education and Employment (DfEE) (nd) Private Finance Division: PFI/PPP project listings, London, DfEE.

Department for Education and Employment (DfEE) (1997a) *Learning to Compete*, London, HMSO.

Department for Education and Employment (DfEE) (1997b) *Qualifying for Success*, London, HMSO.

Department for Education and Employment (DfEE) (1997c) *Excellence in Schools*, London, HMSO.

Department for Education and Employment (DfEE) (1998) *The Learning Age: A*

Renaissance for a New Britain, London: HMSO.

Department for Education and Employment (DfEE) (1999) *Leaning to Succeed, Learning and Skills Council Prospectus*, London, DfEE.

Department for Education and Skills (DfES) (2002) *14–19: Extending Opportunities and Raising Standards: Summary Document*, London, The Stationery Office.

Department for Education and Skills (DfES) (2003a) *Pupil Absence in Schools in England, 2001/02 (Provisional Statistics)*, Statistical First Release, London, DfES.

Department for Education and Skills (DfES) (2003b) *Permanent Exclusions from Schools and Exclusion Appeals in England 2001/2002 (provisional)*, London, DfES.

Department for Education and Skills (DfES) (2003c) *GCE/VCE A/AS Examination Results for Young People in England 2002/2003*, London, DfES accessed online 30 November 2003,
http://www.dfes.gov.uk/rsgateway/DB/SFR/s000475/index.shtml

Department for Education and Skills (DfES) (2003d) *School Workforce Remodelling*, London, DfES, accessed online 23 October 2003,
http://www.teachernet.gov.uk/management/remodelling/

Department for Education and Skills (DfES) (2003e) *21st Century Skills: Realising our Potential*, London, The Stationery Office.

Department for Education and Skills (DfES) (2003f) *The Core Principles: Teaching and Learning; School Improvement; System Wide Reform*, London: DfES.

Department for Education and Skills (DfES) (2003g) *National Statistics First Release. Participation in Education, Training and Employment by 16–18 Year Olds in England 2001 and 2002*, SFR 31/2003, London, HMSO.

Department for Education and Skills (DfES) (2003h) *14–19: Opportunity and Excellence (Summary)*, London, The Stationery Office.

Department for Education and Skills DfES (2004a) 'The standards site: specialist schools', London, DfES, Accessed online 1 July 2004,
http://www.standards.dfes.gov.uk/specialistschools/news/?version=1

Department for Education and Skills (DfES) (2004b) '14–19 Green Paper consultation workshops review', accessed online 8 January 2004,
http://www.des.gov.uk/consultations/sor/sordocs/SOR_208_2.pdf

Department of Education and Science (DES) (1984) *Training for Jobs*, London, HMSO.

Department of Education and Science (DES) (1988) *Advancing A-levels* (Higginson Report) London, HMSO.

Department of Education and Science/Department of Employment (DES/DE) (1991) *Education and Training for the 21st Century*, London, HMSO.

Dweck, C. (1986) 'Motivational processes affecting learning', *American Psychologist*, (special issue: Psychological science and education, vol. 41, pp. 1040–8.

Earley, P., Evans, J., Collarbone, P., Gold, A. and Halpin, D. (2002) *Establishing the Current State of School Leadership in England, Research Brief RB336*, London, DfES.

East Midlands Learning and Skills Research Network (2002) *'My Mates Are Dead Jealous Cause They Don't Get To Come Here!': An Analysis of the Provision of Alternative, Non School-based Learning Activities for 14 to 16 Year-olds in the East Midlands*, Nottingham, LSDA.

Ecclestone, K. (2000) 'Bewitched bothered and bewildered: a policy analysis of the GNVQ assessment regime 1992–2000', *Journal of Education Policy*, vol. 15, no. 5, pp. 539–58, accessed online 19 December 2003,
http://search.epnet.com/direct.asp?an=3847203&db=afh

Ecclestone, K. and Pryor, J. (2003) '"Learning careers" or "assessment careers"? The impact of assessment systems on learning', *British Educational Research Journal*, vol. 29, no. 4, pp. 471–88.

Edem, A., Spencer, P. and Fyfield, B. (2003) *Organisation of Provision of Post-16 Education and Training*, London, DfES and Learning and Skills Development Agency.

Edwards, T. and Whitty, G. (1997) 'Specialisation and selection in secondary education', *Oxford Review of Education*, vol. 23, no. 1, pp. 5–15.

Elbaz, F. (1993) 'Responsive teaching: a response from a teacher's perspective', *Journal of Curriculum Studies*, vol. 215, no. 2, pp. 189–99.

Elias, J.L. (1979) 'Critique: androgogy revisited', *Adult Education*, vol. 29, pp. 252–5.

Elliott, G. and Hall, V. (1994) 'FE Inc. – business orientation in further education and the introduction of human resource management', *School Organisation*, vol. 14, no. 1, pp. 3–10.

Engestrom, Y. (1991) '"*Non Scholae sed Vitae Discimus*": towards overcoming the encapsulation of school learning', *Learning and Instruction*, vol. 1, no. 3. pp. 243–59.

Farley, M. (1985) 'Trends and structural changes in English vocational education', in Dale, R. (ed.) *Education, Training and Employment – Towards a New Vocationalism?*, Oxford, Pergamon Press.

Farnham, D. (1993) *Managing the New Public Services*, London, Macmillan.

Felstead, A. and Unwin, L. (2001) 'Funding post compulsory education and training: a retrospective analysis of the TEC and FEFC systems and their impact on skills', *Journal of Education and Work*, vol. 14, no. 1, pp. 91–111.

Ferguson, R. and Unwin, L. (1996) 'Making better sense of post-16 destinations: a case study of an English shire county', *Research Papers in Education*, vol 11, no. 1 pp. 53–81.

Finegold, D. and Soskice, D. (1988) 'The failure of training in Britain', in Esland, G. (ed.) *Education, Training and Employment*, Milton Keynes, Open University Press.

Foskett, N.H. (1999) 'Strategy, external relations and marketing', in Lumby, J. and Foskett, N.H. (eds) *Managing External Relations in Schools and Colleges*, London, PCP/Sage.

Foskett, N.H. and Hemsley-Brown, J.V. (1999) *Teachers and Careers Education – Teachers' Awareness of Careers Outside Teaching*, Southampton, CREM.

Foskett, N.H. and Hemsley-Brown, J.V. (2001) *Choosing Futures: Young People's Decision-making in Education, Training and Careers Markets*, London, Routledge-Falmer.

Foskett, N.H. and Hesketh, A.J. (1997) 'Constructing choice in contiguous and parallel markets: institutional and school leavers' responses to the new post-16 marketplace', *Oxford Review of Education*, vol. 23, no. 3, pp. 299–330.

Foskett, N. and Lumby, J. (2003) *Leading and Managing Education: International Dimensions*, London, Paul Chapman Publishing.

Foskett, N.H., Dyke, M. and Maringe, F. (2004) *The Influence of the School in the Decision to Participate in Learning Post-16*, London, DfES.

Foskett, N., Lumby, J. and Maringe, F. (2003) 'Pathways and progression at 16+ – 'fashion', peer influence and college choice', paper presented to the Annual Conference of the British Educational Research Association, Heriot-Watt University, Edinburgh, 11 September.

Fouts, J.T. and Chan, J. (1997) 'The development of work-study and school enterprises in China's schools', *Curriculum Studies*, vol. 29, pp. 34–46.

Fullan, M. (2003) *Change Forces with a Vengeance*, London, RoutledgeFalmer.

Furman, G. and Shields, C. (2003) 'How can educational leaders promote and support social justice and democratic community in schools?', paper presented at the American Educational Research Association 2003 Annual Meeting, Chicago, 21–25 April.

Further Education Development Agency (FEDA) (1995) *Mapping the FE Sector*, London, DfEE.

Further Education Unit (FEU) (1979) *A Basis for Choice*, Blagdon, FEU.

Gambetta, D. (1996) *Were They Pushed or Did They Jump? Individual Decision Mechanisms in Education*, Boulder, CO, Westview Press.

Gewirtz, S., Ball, S.J. and Bowe, R. (1995) *Markets, Choice and Equity in Education*, Milton Keynes, Open University Press.

Glatter, R. (1996) 'Managing dilemmas in education: the tightrope walk of strategic choice in autonomous institutions', in Jacobson, S.L., Hickox, E.S. and Stevenson, R.B. (eds) *School Administration: persistent dilemmas in preparational practice*, Westport, CT, Praeger.

Glatter, R. (2003) 'Collaboration, collaboration, collaboration – the origins and implications of a policy', *Management in Education*, vol 17, no. 5, pp. 16–20.

Glatter, R., Woods, P. and Bagley, C. (1997) 'Diversity, differentiation and hierarchy: school choice and parental preference', in Glatter, R., Woods, P. and Bagley, C. (eds) *Choice and Diversity in Schooling: Perspectives and Prospects*, London, Routledge.

Gleeson, D. (1990) 'Skills training and its alternatives', in Gleeson, D. (ed.) *Training and its Alternatives*, Milton Keynes, Open University Press.

Gleeson, D. (1996) 'Continuity and change in post-compulsory education and training reform', in Halsall, R. and Cockett, M. (eds) *Education and Training 14–19: Chaos or Coherence?*, London, David Fulton.

Gleeson, D. (2001) 'Style and substance in education leadership: further education as a case in point', *Journal of Education Policy*, vol. 16, no. 3, 181–96.

Gleeson, D. and Shain, F. (1999) 'Managing ambiguity: between markets and managerialism – a case study of "middle" managers in further education', *Sociological Review*, vol. 47, no. 3, pp. 461–90.

GMB (2003) *Education's Hidden Professionals: GMB National Survey of Teaching Assistants and Nursery Nurses*, London, GMB.

Godfrey, C., Hutton, S., Bradshaw, J., Coles, B., Craig, G. and Johnson, J. (2002) *Estimating the Cost of Being 'Not in Education, Employment or Training' at Age 16–18*, London, DfES.

Goldstein, H. (2001) 'Using pupil performance data for judging schools and teachers: scope and limitations', *British Educational Research Journal*, vol. 27, no. 4, pp. 433–42.

Gorard, S. and Taylor, C. (2001) 'The composition of specialist schools in England: track record and future performance', *School Leadership and Management*, vol. 21, no. 4. pp. 365–81.

Gorard, S., Fitz, J. and Taylor, C. (2003) *Schools, Markets and Choice Policies*, London, RoutledgeFalmer.

Goulding, J., Dominey, J. and Gray, M. (1998) *Hard Nosed Decisions: Planning Human Resources in FE*, London, FEDA.

Griffiths, M. (2000) 'Collaboration and partnership in question: knowledge, politics and practice', *Journal of Education Policy*, vol. 15, no. 4, pp. 383–95.

Gronn, P. (2000) 'Distributed properties: a new architecture for leadership', paper presented at BEMAS Research 2000, 'Leading educational management in learning societies: research, policy and practice', the 6th International Educational Management and Administration Research Conference, 29–31 March, Robinson College, University of Cambridge.

Hall, V. (1999) 'Partnerships, alliances and competition: defining the field', in Lumby, J. and Foskett, N. (eds) *Managing External Relations in Schools and Colleges*, London, Paul Chapman Publishing.

Hallinger, P. and Heck, R. (1996) 'The principal's role in school effectiveness: an assessment of methodological progress, 1980–1995', in Leithwood, K., Chapman, J., Corson, D., Hallinger, P. and Hart, A. (eds) *International Handbook of Educational Leadership and Administration*, vol. 2, London, Kluwer Academic.

Handy, C. (1994) *The Empty Raincoat*, London, Hutchinson.

Hanson, E.M. and Henry, W. (1992) 'Strategic marketing for educational systems', *School Organisation*, vol.12, no. 2, pp. 255–67.

Hargreaves, D. (2003) *Education Epidemic: Transforming Secondary Schools through Innovation Networks*, London, DEMOS.

Harris, A. (2004) 'Distributed leadership and school improvement: leading or misleading?', *Educational Management and Administration*, vol. 32, no. 1, pp. 11–24.

Harris, S., Wallace, G. and Rudduck, J. (1995) '"It's not that I haven't learned much. It's just that I really don't understand what I 'm doing": metacognition and secondary-school students', *Research Papers in Education*, vol. 10, no. 2, pp. 253–71.

Hemsley-Brown, J.V. (1999) 'College choice: perceptions and priorities', *Educational Management and Administration*, vol. 27, no. 1 pp. 85–98.

Hemsley-Brown, J.V. and Foskett, N.H. (2000) *Factors Affecting Post-16 Choices in Inner London*, London, FOCUS TEC.

Hewitt, P. and Crawford M. (1997) 'Introducing new contracts: managing change in the context of an enterprise culture', in Levačić, R. and Glatter, R. (eds) 'Managing change in further education', *FEDA Report*, vol. 1, no. 7.

Higham, J., Sharp, P. and Yeomans, D. (1996) *The Emerging 16–19 Curriculum*, London, David Fulton.

Higham, J., Haynes, G., Wragg, C. and Yeomans, D. (2004) '14–19 Pathfinders: an evaluation of the first year. Summary', accessed online 26 May 2004, http://www.dfes.gov.uk/14–19/dsp_evaluation

Hillier, J. (1996) 'Introduction', GNVQ research conference NCVQ, 11 December, Royal Institute of British Architects, London.

Hodgson-Wilson, E.J. (2004) 'Policy espousal, policy enactment and policy experienced: a study of the origins, tensions and contradictions embedded in the development of GNVQs between 1992–2000 in relation to student progression', unpublished PhD thesis, University of Southampton.

Hodgson, A. and Spours, K. (eds) (1997) *Dearing and Beyond: 14–19 Qualifications and Frameworks*, London, Kogan Page.

Hodgson, A. and Spours, K. (1999) *New Labour's Educational Agenda: Issues and Policies for Education and Training from 14+*, London, Kogan Page.

Hodgson, A. and Spours, K. (2001) 'Part-time work and full-time education in the UK: the emergence of a curriculum and policy issue', *Journal of Education and*

Work, vol. 14, no. 3, pp. 373–88.

Hodgson, A. and Spours, K. (2002) 'Key skills for all? The key skills qualification and curriculum 2000', *Journal of Education Policy*, vol. 17, no. 1, pp. 29–47.

Hodgson, A. and Spours, K. (2003) *Beyond A Levels: Curriculum and the Reform of 14–19 Qualifications*, London, Kogan Page.

Hodkinson, P. (1998) 'Choosing GNVQ', *Journal of Education and Work*, vol. 11, no. 2, pp. 151–65.

Hodkinson, P. and Sparkes, A. (1997) 'Careership: a sociological theory of career decision-making', *British Journal of Sociology of Education*, vol. 10, no. 1, pp. 23–35.

Hughes, C. (1997) *Lessons Are for Learning*, Stafford, Network Educational Press.

Hughes, C. (1999) 'Teenagers learning and earning', press release, 15 July, London, FEDA.

Huxham, C. and Vangen, S. (2000) 'What makes partnerships work?', in Osborne, S. (ed.) *Public–Private Partnerships; Theory and Practice in International Perspective*, London, Routledge.

Institute for Public Policy Research (IPPR) (1990) *A British Baccalaureate: Ending the Division between Education and Training*, London, IPPR.

Janis, I. and Mann, L. (1977) *Decision-Making: A Psychological Analysis of Conflict, Choice and Commitment*, New York, Macmillan.

Jarvis, P., Holford, J. and Griffin, C. (2003) *The Theory and Practice of Learning*, London, Kogan Page.

Jessup, G. (1991) *Outcomes: NVQs and the Emerging Model of Education and Training*, London, Falmer Press.

Keep, E. (1999) 'UK's VET policy and the "Third Way": following a high skills trajectory or running up a dead end street?', *Journal of Education and Work*, vol. 12, no. 3. pp. 323–46.

Kennedy, H. (1997) *Learning Works: Widening Participation in Further Education* (Kennedy Report), Coventry, FEFC.

Keys, W. and Maychell, K., with Evans, C., Brooks. R., Lee, B. and Pathak, S. (1998) *Staying On: A Study of Young People's Decisions about School Sixth Forms, Sixth-form Colleges and Colleges of Further Education*, Slough, NFER.

King, K. (1993) 'Technical and vocational education and training in an international context', *Vocational Aspect of Education*, vol. 45, pp. 201–16.

Kingston, P. (2004) 'Converted to the cause', *Education Guardian*, 29 June 2004, p. 16.

Lave, J. and Wenger, E. (1990). *Situated Learning: Legitimate Peripheral Participation*,. Cambridge, Cambridge University Press.

Le Grand, J. (1990) *Quasi Markets and Social Policy*, Bristol, University of Bristol.

Lepkowska, D. (2004) 'Kept afloat by parents', *Times Educational Supplement*, 2 January.

Levačić, R. and Glover, D. (1997) 'Value for money as a school improvement strategy: evidence from the new inspection system in England', *School Effectiveness and School Improvement*, vol. 8, no. 2, pp. 231–53.

Levačić, R. and Vignoles, A. (2002) 'Researching the links between school resources and student outcomes in the UK: a review of issues and evidence', *Education Economics*, vol. 10, no. 3, pp. 313–31.

Levin, B. (2003) 'Educational policy: commonalities and differences', in Davies, B. and West-Burnham, J. (eds) *Handbook of Educational Leadership and Management*, London, Pearson.

Levin, J. (2001) *Globalizing the Community College*, New York, Palgrave.

Lowndes, V. and Skelcher, C. (1998) 'The dynamics of multi-organizational part-nership: an analysis of changing modes of governance', *Public Administration*, vol. 76, pp. 313–33.

Lucas, R. and Lammont, N. (1998) 'Combining work and study: an empirical study of full-time students in school, college and university', *Journal of Education and Work*, vol. 11, no. 1 pp. 41–56.

Lumby, J. (1996) 'Curriculum change in further education', *Vocational Aspect of Education*, vol. 48, no. 4, pp. 333–48.

Lumby, J. (2001a) 'Framing learning and teaching for the 21st century', in Middlewood, D. and Burton, N. (eds) *Managing the Curriculum*, London, Paul Chapman Publishing.

Lumby, J. (2001b) *Managing Further Education Colleges: Learning Enterprise*, London, Paul Chapman Publishing.

Lumby, J. (2003a) 'Constructing culture change: the case of sixth form colleges', *Educational Management and Administration*, vol. 31, no. 2, pp. 157–72.

Lumby, J. (2003b) 'Distributed leadership in colleges: leading or misleading?', *Educational Management and Administration*, vol. 31, no. 3, pp. 283–93.

Lumby, J. and Briggs, A.R.J., with Wilson, M., Glover, D. and Pell, A. (2002) *Sixth Form Colleges: Policy, Purpose and Practice*, Leicester, Leicester University.

Lumby, J. and Morrison, M. (2004) *Local Evaluation of Boston College 14–19 Pathfinder Partnership*, Lincoln, University of Lincoln.

Lumby, J. and Wilson, M. (2003) 'Developing 14–19 education: meeting needs and improving choice', *Journal of Education Policy*, vol. 18, no. 5, pp. 533–50.

Lumby, J., Foskett, N. and Maringe, F. (2003a) *Choice, Pathways and Progression for Young People in London West: A Report to London West Learning and Skills Council*, London LWLSC.

Lumby, J., Foskett, N. and Maringe, F. (2003b) 'Restricted view: school leadership and the "choices" of learners', paper presented to the Annual Conference of the British Educational, Leadership and Management Society, Milton Keynes, 3–5 October.

Lutz, F. (1988) 'Strategy formation in the university setting', in Westoby, A. (ed.) *Culture and Power in Educational Organizations*, Milton Keynes, Open University Press.

Manpower Services Commission (MSC) (1977) *Young People and Work* (Holland Report), London, HMSO.

Manpower Services Commission (MSC) (1981) *A New Training Initiative: An Agenda for Action*, London, HMSO.

Marples, R. (1996) '14–19', in Docking, J. (ed.) *National School Policy: Major issues in Education Policy for Schools in England and Wales, 1979 onwards*, London, David Fulton.

Mayne, P. (1992) 'Teaching and learning styles', in Whiteside, T., Sutton, A. and Everton, T. (eds) *16–19 Changes in Education and Training*, London, David Fulton.

McDonald, J. and Lucas, N. (2001) 'The impact of FEFC funding 1997–99: research on 14 colleges', *Journal of Further and Higher Education*, vol. 25, no. 2, pp. 215–26.

McLean, M. (1995) *Educational Traditions Compared: Content, Teaching and Learning in Industrialised Countries*, London, David Fulton.

McQuaid, R. (2000) 'The theory of partnership; why have partnerships?', in

Osborne, S. (ed.) *Public–Private Partnerships: Theory and Practice in International Perspective*, London, Routledge.

Minton, D. (1991) *Teaching Skills in Further and Adult Education*, Basingstoke, City and Guilds/Macmillan.

Mordaunt, E. (1999) '"Not for Wimps": the nature of partnership', paper presented at the British Educational Research Association Conference, Brighton, September.

Morgan, G. (1986) *Images of Organization*, London, Sage.

Morris, M., Nelson, J., Rickinson, M., Storey, S. and Benfield, P. (1999) *A literature review of young people's attitudes to education, employment and training, Research Report 170*, Sheffield, DEE.

Morris, R. (1994) 'New magistracies and commissariats', *Local Government Studies*, vol. 20, no. 2, pp.57–85.

Mortimore, P. (1999) 'Pedagogy: what do we know?', in Mortimore, P. (ed.) *Understanding Pedagogy and its Impact on Learning*, London, Paul Chapman Publishing.

Moynagh, M. and Worsley, R. (2003) *Learning from the Future: Scenarios for Post-16 Learning*, Wellington: Learning and Skills Research Centre.

National Advisory Group for Continuing Education and Lifelong Learning (1997) *Learning for the Twenty-first Century: First Report of the National Advisory Group for Continuing Education and Lifelong Learning* (Fryer Report), London, NAGCELL.

National Curriculum Council (NCC) (1990) *Core Skills 16–19*, York, NCC.

Nicholls, A. (1994) *Schools and Colleges: Collaborators or Competitors in Education?*, London, LASER FE Council.

Noble, T. and Pym, B. (1989) 'Collegial authority and the receding locus of power', in Bush, T. (ed.) *Managing Education: Theory and Practice*, Milton Keynes, Open University Press.

O'Hear, A. (1991) *Education and Democracy against the Educational Establishment*, London: Claridge.

Office for Standards in Education (OFSTED) (2003) *Annual report of Her Majesty's Chief Inspector of Schools. Standards and Quality in Education 2001/02*, London, DFES, accessed online 8 September 2003, http://www.ofsted.gov.uk/publications/docs/3150.doc

Organization for Economic Cooperation and Development (OECD) (1992) *High Quality Education and Training for All*, Paris, OECD.

Paechter, C. (2001) 'Schooling and the ownership of knowledge', in Paechter, C., Preedy, M., Scott, D. and Soler, J. (eds) *Knowledge, Power and Learning*, London, Paul Chapman Publishing.

Palmer, G., Carr, J., North, J. and Kenway, P. (2003) *Monitoring Poverty and Social Exclusion*, London, Joseph Rowntree Foundation, accessed online 14 June 2004, http://www.poverty.org.uk/reports/mp2003.pdf

Paterson, L. and Raffe, D. (1995) '"Staying on" in full time education in Scotland, 1985–1991', *Oxford Review of Education*, vol. 21, no. 1, pp. 3–23.

Payne, J. (2002) *Choice at the End of Compulsory Schooling: A Research Review*, London, DfES.

Payne, J. (2003) 'The impact of part-time jobs in years 12 and 13 on qualification achievement', *British Educational Research Journal*, vol. 29, no. 4, pp. 599–611.

Perry, A. (1997) *A Pencil Instead: Why We Need a New Funding System for Further*

Education, London, Lambeth College.

Piore, D. and Sabel, C. (1984) *The Second Industrial Divide*, New York, Basic Books.

Pring, R. (1990) *The New Curriculum*, London, Cassell.

Pring, R. (1995) *Closing the Gap: Liberal Education and Vocational Preparation*, London, Hodder and Stoughton.

Raffe, D. (1985) 'Education and training initiatives for 14–18s: content and context', in Watts, A.G. (ed.) *Education and Training 14–18: Policy and Practice*, Cambridge, CRAC.

Raffe, D. (2002) 'The issues, some reflections and possible next steps, in 14–19 education', paper arising from a seminar series held at the Nuffield Foundation, December 2001–January 2002, London, Nuffield Foundation, accessed on line 30 June 2002, http//.www.nuffieldfoundation.org

Raffo, C. (2003) 'Disaffected young people and the work-related curriculum at Key Stage 4: issues of social capital development and learning as a form of cultural practice', *Journal of Education and Work*, vol. 16, no. 1, pp. 69–86.

Raggett, P. (1994) 'Implementing NVQs in colleges: progress, perceptions and issues', *Journal of Further and Higher Education*, vol. 18, no. 1, pp. 59–74.

Rajan, A., Van Eupen, P. and Jaspers, A. (1997) *Britain's Flexible Labour Market: What Next?* London: DfEE.

Reay, D. (2001a) 'Finding or losing yourself? Working class relationships to education', *Journal of Education Policy*, vol. 17, no. 1, pp. 29–47.

Reay, D. (2001b) 'Finding or losing yourself? Working class relationships to education', *Journal of Education Policy*, vol. 16, no. 4, pp. 333–46.

Salter, B. and Tapper, T. (eds) (1981) *Education, Politics and the State: The Theory and Practice of Educational change*, London: Grant McIntyre.

Schagen, I. and Schagen, S. (2003) 'Analysis of national value-added datasets to estimate the impact of specialist schools on pupil performances', *Educational Studies*, vol. 29, no. 1, pp. 3–18.

Schagen, S., Johnson, F. and Simkin, C. (1996) *Sixth Form Options – Post-compulsory Education in Maintained Schools*, Slough, NFER.

Schein, E.H. (1997) *Organizational Culture and Leadership*, 2nd edn, San Francisco, CA, Jossey-Bass.

Scrimshaw, P. (1983) *Purpose and Planning in the Classroom*, Milton Keynes, Open University Press.

Shah, C. (2003) 'Employment shifts in the technical and further education workforce, *Education Economics*, vol. 11, no. 2, pp. 193–208.

Shain, F. (1999) 'Managing to lead: women managers in the further education sector', paper presented at the BERA annual conference, University of Sussex, Brighton, 2–5 September.

Shepherd, G. (1994) 'Foreword by the Secretary of State', in *Education Means Business: Private Finance in Education*, London, Department for Education.

Shorter, P. (1994) 'Sixth-form colleges and incorporation: some evidence from case studies in the north of England', *Oxford Review of Education*, vol. 20, no. 4, pp. 461–73.

Simkins, T. (2000) 'Education reform and managerialism: comparing the experience of school and colleges', *Journal of Education Policy*, vol. 15, no. 3, pp. 317–32.

Smithers, A. (1994) *All our Futures* (Channel Four 'Dispatches' television programme).

Steedman, H. (2002) 'Employers, employment and the labour market, in 14–19 education', paper arising from a seminar series held at the Nuffield Foundation, December 2001–January 2002, London, Nuffield Foundation, accessed online 30 June 2002, http//.www.nuffieldfoundation.org

Stefani, L.A.J. (1994) 'Peer, self and tutor assessment: relative reliabilities', *Studies in Higher Education*, vol. 19, pp. 69–75.

Stewart, W., Wright, G. and Slater, J. (2004) 'Schools sound alarm over funding', *Times Educational Supplement*, 23 January 2004.

Stillman, A. and Maychell, K. (1986) *Moving to Secondary School. Who Decides? A Questionnaire for Parents*, Slough, NFER/Nelson

Stoll, L. and Fink, D. (1996) *Changing our Schools*, Buckingham, Open University Press.

Storey, J. (1998) 'HR and organizational structure', *Financial Times 'Mastering Management' Review*, vol. 17, pp. 40–3.

Tait, T., Frankland, G., Smith, D. and Moore, S. (2002) *Curriculum 2000+2: Tracking Institutions' and Learners' Experiences*, London, LSDA.

Task Group on Assessment and Testing (TGAT) (1987) *A Report*, London, DES.

Tawney, R.H. (1938) *Religion and the Rise of Capitalism: An Historical Study*, London, Penguin.

Taylor, A. (1998) 'Employability skills: from corporate "wish list" to government policy', *Journal of Curriculum Studies*, vol. 30, no. 2, pp. 143–64.

Temple, H. (1991) *Open Learning in Industry, Developing Flexibility and Competence in the Workforce*, Harlow, Longman.

Thomson, A. (2004) 'Big questions, big answers', *FE Now*, Summer, pp. 16–17.

Thomas D. (1995) 'Learning to be flexible', in Thomas D. (ed.) *Flexible Learning Strategies in Higher and Further Education*, London, Cassell.

Thomas, S., Smees, R., MacBeath, J. and Robertson, P. (2000) 'Valuing pupils' views in Scottish schools', *Educational Research and Evaluation*, vol. 6, no. 4, pp. 281–316.

Thomas, W., Webber, D.J. and Walton, F. (2002) 'The school leaving intentions at the age of sixteen: evidence from a multicultural city environment', *Economic Issues*, vol. 7, no. 1, pp. 1–14.

Thrupp, M. (1998) 'The art of the possible: organizing high and low socioeconomic Schools', *Journal of Educational Policy*, vol. 13, no. 2, pp. 197–219.

Torrance, H. (1993) 'Formative assessment: some theoretical problems and empirical questions', *Cambridge Journal of Education*, vol. 23, no. 3, pp. 333–44.

Torrance, H. and Coultas, J. (2004) *Do Summative Assessment and Testing Have a Positive or Negative Effect on Post-16 Learners' Motivation for Learning in the Learning and Skills Sector?*, London, Learning and Skills Research Centre.

Tuckett, A. (1997) *Life Long Learning in England and Wales: An Overview and Guide to Issues Arising from the European Year of Lifelong Learning*, Leicester, NIACE.

Tunstall, P. (2003) 'Definitions of the "subject": the relations between the discourses of educational assessment and the psychology of motivation and their constructions of personal reality', *British Education Research Journal*, vol. 29, no. 4, pp. 505–20.

Unwin, L. (2002) 'Young people, transitions and progression, paper arising from a seminar series held at the Nuffield Foundation, December 2001–January 2002, London, Nuffield Foundation, accessed online 30 June 2002, http//.www.nuffieldfoundation.org

Walford, G. (2000) 'From city technology colleges to sponsored grant-maintained schools', *Oxford Review of Education*, vol. 26, no. 2, pp. 145–58.

Ward, L. (2003) 'NUT members in classroom assistants boycott', *Guardian*, 7 October.

Watkins, C. and Mortimore, P. (1999) 'Pedagogy: what do we know?', in Mortimore, P. (ed.) *Understanding Pedagogy and its Impact on Learning*, London, Paul Chapman Publishing.

Watts, A.G. and Young, M. (1997) 'Models of student guidance in a changing 14–19 education and training system', in Edwards, R., Harrison, R. and Tait, A. (eds) *Telling Tales: Perspectives on Guidance and Counselling in Learning*, London, Routledge.

West, A. and Pennel, H. (2000) 'New Labour and school-based education in England: changing the system of funding', *British Education Research Journal*, vol. 26, no. 4. pp. 523–36.

Williams, M. (1992) 'Ruskin in context', in Williams, M., Daugherty, R. and Burns, F. (eds) *Continuing the Education Debate*, London, Cassell.

Willis, P. (1987) 'Foreword', in Finn, D. (ed.) *Training without Jobs: New Deals and Broken Promises*, London, Macmillan.

Wolf, A. (1998) 'Portfolio assessment as national policy; the National Council for Vocational Qualifications and its quest for pedagogical revolution', *Assessment in Education: Principles, Policy and Practice*, vol. 5, no. 3, pp. 413–46.

Wolf, A. (2002) *Does Education Matter? Myths about Education and Economic Growth*, London, Penguin.

Wolf, A. and Black, H. (1990) *Knowledge and Competence: Current Issues in Training and Education*, Sheffield, Careers and Occupational Information Centre.

Woods, P. and Levačić, R. (2002) 'Raising school performance in the league tables (part 1): disentangling the effects of social disadvantage', *British Educational Research Journal*, vol. 28, no.2, pp. 207–26.

Woods, P., Bagley, C. and Glatter, R. (1998) *School Choice and Competition: Markets in the Public Interest?*, London, Routledge.

Working Group on 14–19 Reform (2003) '14–19 Green Paper consultation workshops review', accessed online 8 January 2004, http://www.des.gov.uk/consultations/sor/sordocs/SOR_208_2.pdf

Working Group on 14–19 Reform (2004) *14–19 Curriculum and Qualifications Reform [Electronic Resource]: Interim Report of the Working Group on 14–19 Reform*, London, DfES.

Wyn, J. and Dwyer, P. (1999) 'New directions in research on youth in transition', *Journal of Youth Studies*, vol. 2, no. 1, pp. 5–21.

Young, M. (1996) 'A curriculum for the twenty-first century? Towards a new basis for overcoming academic/vocational divisions', in Ahier, J., Cosin, B. and Hales, M. (eds) *Diversity and Change: Education Policy and Selection*, London: Routledge.

10 Downing Street. (2004) 'GCSE results improving', accessed online 11 February 2004, http://www.number-10.gov.uk/output/Page4618.asp

Author index

Subject index